God's \

John H Price

British Library Cataloguing in Publication Data
A catalogue record for this book is available from the British Library

ISBN 978-1-4452-7949-7

Cover image by Eric Gavaert

Printed in Great Britain

Contents

Getting Started

A Palm Beach........

I remember it still. Not some exotic location on distant shores but the name of my first bike. It was blue with two palm trees painted on the cross bar. My parents knew someone who knew someone else who had a bike for sale. It was of no consequence whatsoever to me that in today's terminology, it was 'pre-owned'. I loved it, rode it everywhere. As a 12 year old, I would spend whole days in the summer holidays 'off on my bike'.

My first 'wheels'.

Motor scooters came next.

My first was a very old Lambretta, which was quite a challenge to ride because it had the headlight on the front fixed fairing instead of on the handlebars. That proved to be a problem going round corners. You were round the corner before the light from the headlight caught up. It wasn't too much of a problem, however, because it was so slow. I soon determined that speed was important so my next scooter was a Lambretta TV 175.

I was visiting an Art Gallery recently and standing in the corner was a TV 125cc, which had belonged to some 60's rock-star. Mine was a 175cc. It was quick – relatively speaking, of course - when compared to the Palm Beach, with a headlight on the handlebars for going around corners much faster. It also had a double saddle. A double saddle was a new innovation – it replaced two separate seats – and was much cosier if you had that 'special person' as pillion.

My 'special person', of whom I will write in later chapters, fell off that motor scooter on our very first outing. A car coming in the opposite direction took the bend in the road too sharply and forced me into a ditch. The only damage was my pride and her laddered stockings but I realized that I needed something more sophisticated. Sophistication came in the form of an old Mini, white with a black roof and red seats. In the looks department it was passable but on the road it was also passable – and everyone did!

Being creative in my thinking, especially when it came to cars, I had other ideas. A specialist engine tuner was the solution. He agreed to replace the 850cc engine with a new 1100cc one. His words to me were, 'It will fly!' but unfortunately it flew like a lame duck. Months later and after considerable expense, I discovered it wasn't a new engine, it wasn't 1100cc and it wasn't fitted correctly. So my love affair with cars – excitement and heartbreak – began.

Dear Reader - you are already beginning to get the drift that I have always loved 'wheels' - push bikes, motor scooters, cars. They all have wheels and I love them. For some people, 'wheels' are simply a means of getting from A to B but for me, and I suspect many others, the process of getting from A to B on my 'wheels' is a joy.

I love driving.

I also love God.

I have loved God since the days of my Palm Beach. My love for God – and His amazing love for me - has shaped my whole life and meant that I led 'The Church at Junction 10' in Walsall for 30 years. But can a man love 'God' and 'wheels'? Surely these two 'loves' are incompatible, sharing different worlds?

The Lord and Lambrettas must fit into separate compartments of my living because there is no possible link between someone so infinite and majestic and glorious – and something as mundane as 'wheels'.

However, while reading my Bible, I began to stumble over verses that indicated something different. The Bible took me on an amazing journey.

Deuteronomy 33:27 is a verse that I have used many times, particularly at funeral services. *"The eternal God is your refuge, and underneath are the everlasting arms"*. It's a lovely verse of comfort and reassurance and part of the 'God' compartment of my life. However, if you read the preceding verse, you are suddenly confronted with something that could fit into the 'other' compartment. *"There is no one like the God of Jeshurun, who rides the heavens to help you ..... "*

'How amazing', I thought to myself, 'Is the God who rides the heavens ready to come to my rescue?' I have been rescued several times by AA and RAC and Green Flag personnel so the concept of the Lord God Almighty riding to my rescue was thought provoking. The idea of God riding anything is captivating but Moses says that He rides 'the heavens'. How magnificent is this Lord of ours! A link, however tenuous, began to form in mind between God and the ever so mundane subject of 'wheels'.

Please relax because I'm not talking about toe curling jokes that ask what motor-bike God rides? 'He rides in Triumph ....'

No, I'm asking if the Lord of All Creation has an understanding of something so ordinary in my life - my love for 'wheels'. The question is asked reverently but is the Lord interested in my transport?

He rides the heavens; is He interested in what I ride or drive? If He is, then I begin to perceive that nothing in my day-to-day, ordinary living falls outside His understanding. *'His eye is on the sparrow'* may be wonderfully heart-warming to twitchers but the possibility that He knows all about 'wheels' is even more wonderful to me – and, I suspect, to others.

So I began a journey and you are invited to motor along with me.

I want to share from the Bible God's interest in wheels. Alongside that I want to share the story of how 'The Church at Junction 10' came to be. Our journey winds its way mainly through the pages of the Old Testament, stopping off at some quite unexpected places, before coming to an end in the New Testament. It also spends time in a town called Walsall.

In the early 1980's I was preaching in Rock Church, Manhattan, New York, just around the corner from Central Park. Introducing myself, I told them I was from a church in Walsall. At the end of our first service, an elderly American gentleman ambled over to me and said, 'Gee – you speak great English for a Polack!' So to avoid similar confusion, this is Walsall in the West Midlands, not Warsaw, Poland!

So, without more ado, let's get started!

Section One

Jacob

Chapter 1

In The Cart

Dolly was a large black carthorse.

She seemed large to me because I was a six year old keen to help my granddad. At the end of his working day as a mobile greengrocer, he would remove Dolly's harness and bridle and lead her from between the shafts of the cart. Then he would lift me up and put me on her back. Slapping her rump, he'd give her the word to go to her field, some half a mile distant.

Riding bareback and alone on this gentle, lumbering carthorse was one of the delights of my childhood. I felt very grown up being in charge of this big black horse. Just holding onto her mane, I sat as she slowly made her own way to the field. Once there, I'd slide off her back, open the gate and she would make her way through.

I was born in a village called Gornal in the West Midlands of the United Kingdom. When I was young, as well as having lots to do with horses and carts, I remember a strange expression my parents often used. If someone was in trouble they would say, 'Now he's in the cart.' It meant you were in big trouble. Research indicates that it almost certainly refers back to the French Revolution. The French aristocracy were loaded into open carts called tumbrels and taken to be executed at the guillotine in Paris. For these poor unfortunates 'in the cart' meant imminent death.

Our first section is all about you 'being in the cart' but it's nothing to lose your head about. It represents a place of imminent blessing. It's a place where you experience the grace and favour of God.

I have experienced that!

Together with Judith, my wife, we have experienced the grace and favour of God as we led 'The Church at Junction 10' in Walsall for over 30 years. It began with the aim of simply preaching the gospel to bring people to know Jesus. As a 'new' church, we didn't have a church building. To be fair, we didn't have anything – no money, no experience, no wealthy 'backers', no Bible College training and no real perception of what we were about. However, we did know that God had 'called' us to Walsall to plant a church, so we went.

In 1978 we hired a school building. Calling ourselves 'Walsall Evangelistic Centre' – the little church began. It was such a big name for such a tiny group of people. Beginning with just 8 people, we saw God slowly but surely grow the church until several hundred people were associated with us. Some years ago, we decided to change the church's name as we found that people couldn't say, spell or even knew what 'evangelistic' meant. I had some wonderful conversations with the local press, who were running adverts for us, as they stumbled over the word 'evangelistic'. I also got addressed as 'Pasta' on several occasions.

The Church at Junction 10

Taking the lead from Pastor Jack Hayford in California, who called their church 'The Church on the Way', we chose to rename ours: 'The Church at Junction 10'. It was simply stating the obvious - our church lies right on Junction 10 of the M6 motorway, one of the busiest junctions in the UK. Our location has been a great benefit as people travel long distances to fellowship with us, often using the motorway network. It also proved to be a great advantage to car thieves on more than one occasion as they stole our church minibuses. It was so easy for them to quickly get onto the M6 and disappear.

One morning all our church staff was evacuated by the police because they suspected that the IRA had parked a lorry loaded with explosives just off Junction 10. That turned out to be a false alarm but on another occasion, the decomposed body they discovered in the field between us and the motorway was real enough. Apparently, it was a 'gentleman of the road' who had tragically ended his life's journey at Junction 10. He may well have been one of the many 'travellers' who over the years have knocked on our doors, asking for help - and got it.

Although this poor man finished his life journey at Junction 10, many, many other people have begun their walk with God at the Church at Junction 10. It has been an amazing journey, travelled in the company of some great people, whom God sent to help us. He has been so gracious to us but that doesn't mean that it hasn't, at times, been a very difficult journey. As we travel together through this book in wagons and carts, I'll share some of our 'highs and lows' but for now, back to carts.

It's Joseph who is first into carts.

Not until we are well into the story of Joseph do we get the first mention of a cart in the Bible. All carts in the Old Testament were probably of Egyptian origin. They had cornered the cart market because no one else made them as there were no roads and it was more usual to transport people and goods by donkey or camel. Each cart comprised two or three planks of wood that formed the floor, attached to solid wooden wheels, usually two but occasionally four. Generally speaking, chariots were drawn by horses and carts drawn by oxen.

If you ever have the privilege of buying a new car, the salesman will run through all the options available to you, asking what 'extras' you want – metallic paint, alloys, extended warranty, etc. When ordering your new cart from Egypt, you could add just one extra. If you were carrying passengers, it could be fitted with a canopy to protect them from the sun. If you have watched Westerns and seen the early pioneers crossing America in covered wagons, you have an idea of what Bible carts looked like.

Whilst writing this book, I spent some time in India and was amazed to see ox carts that were exactly the same as the ones Joseph used to bring his father Jacob and their wives and children to Egypt. Nothing about them had changed. It brought Genesis 45:19 to life.

> *"Pharaoh said to Joseph, You are directed to tell (your brothers) 'Do this: Take some carts from Egypt for your children and your wives, and get your father and come. Never mind about your belongings, because the best of all Egypt will be yours. So the sons of Israel did this. Joseph gave them carts, as Pharaoh had commanded.*
>
> *So they went up out of Egypt and came to their father Jacob in the land of Canaan. They told him, Joseph is still alive! In fact, he is ruler of all Egypt. Jacob was stunned; he did not believe them. But when they told him everything Joseph had said to them, and when he saw the carts Joseph had sent to carry him back the spirit of their father Jacob revived. And Israel said, 'I'm convinced! My son Joseph is still alive. I will go and see him before I die' "*

As I read these verses, I was strangely impacted. These are the Bible's first 'wheels' and with my interest in all things 'motorized', they set me off on a journey that eventually resulted in this book.

Joseph sent carts for Jacob.

Genesis 45 does say that - but what does that have to do with people of the 21st century?

Before trying to answer that question, let me run through the people taking part. There are three main characters in this story – Joseph, Jacob and Pharaoh.

Pharaoh owns the carts.
Joseph sends them.
Jacob rides in them.

God is about to 'borrow' Pharaoh's wheels for His own use. Isn't that something? How often have I borrowed someone's car or van or lorry to do a job or to make a journey. Here God is doing what we would do in our 21st century world. As I read about the God of All Creation borrowing someone else's 'wheels', it projected a relevancy and application to our everyday living.

This story holds surprise after surprise in what it teaches us about God's plans for us but – first – the background.

Chapter 2

On Your Toes

Three times, Joseph's father Jacob has to run to save his life.

Ezekial Aikle is buried in East Dalhousie Cemetery, Nova Scotia. On his gravestone are these words:

> Here lies
> Ezekial Aikle
> Age 102
> The good
> Die young

Dying at 102, Ezekial was neither young nor good and neither was Jacob. He was a kind of Del Boy Trotter from 'Only Fools and Horses', always fooling someone to get what he wanted. His 'deals' so upset others that he has to run for his life.

First, he runs away from his elder brother, Esau.

In Old Testament times, it was custom and practice for a father to pass on a special blessing to his eldest son. In this family's case, the recipient should have been Esau but Jacob tricks his father Isaac into giving him the blessing instead.

It was a brilliantly engineered sting put together by Jacob and his mother, Rebekah. Esau is furious when he discovers what has taken place and consoles himself with the thought of killing his younger brother. Some years earlier, Jacob had already stolen the birthright from Esau. Birthright was the right of the son born first to inherit a double share of the family wealth but it also carried spiritual privilege. The inheritor would be part of the family tree of the promised Christ. Jacob had talked Esau into trading the birthright for a bowl of broth and now, with his mother's connivance, father Isaac is fooled and the earlier 'trade' bears fruit. It is now all his!

Isaac blesses Jacob as if he were the eldest son – he gets a 'double share' blessing and his name in the genealogy of Jesus. Brother Esau, the victim of the sting, is incensed, incandescent with rage. For Jacob, it's time to vanish. Escape is the only option so Rebekah points him in the direction of his uncle Laban in Haran, from where Granddad Abraham came. Jacob is up on his toes and he's legging it out of there. These 21st century slang expressions make it clear how he escaped - on foot. That is significant.

Secondly, Jacob runs from Laban.

As he arrives at the Laban encampment after a long journey, Jacob has no idea that one day he will have to run away from here too. Jacob reaches Haran and stays with his uncle Laban. On arrival, he meets his cousin, Rachel, who was absolutely stunning. Jacob is so besotted with this lovely young woman that Laban is able to turn the tables on Jacob so now it's his uncle's turn to engineer a sting.

Jacob agrees to works seven years for Rachel's hand in marriage. Genesis 29:17 says that *"Rachel was lovely in form and beautiful"*. He's head over heels in love with her and is happy to work seven years for her but on his wedding night, uncle Laban substitutes Leah for Rachel. Leah is the older, ugly sister that Laban is keen to marry off first. It says that *"Leah had weak eyes"* but Jacob must have had weak eyes too if he couldn't tell the difference between the two. However, the wedding feast maybe left him a little inebriated. Drink can get you into all kinds of trouble; in this case, marrying the wrong wife. Whatever the reason he was fooled and has to work another seven years for Rachel, fourteen in total, although he gets to marry her the next week.

I turned my head to look backwards and processing down the church aisle was the most beautiful woman I have even seen in my life. She stopped as she reached my side and we turned to look at the minister who would marry us. She has stayed by my side for 40 years and to me she still is the most beautiful of women. Like Jacob, I knew all about being besotted and 'worshipped from afar' the young Miss Judith Brookes.

As a 15 year old, I had just two prayers. 'Lord, I want to serve you, wherever, whatever, whenever!' The second prayer didn't have the same 'spiritual' ring to it. I wanted God to fix it for me to go out with the most beautiful young woman in our church. One request was spiritual, the other carnal or so I thought until one Sunday morning. There have been a few times in my long walk with God when He has spoken so clearly that even I could not misunderstand what was being said. This was to be one of those moments.

I was brought up in Eve Lane Pentecostal Church. Frequently, the gifts of the Holy Spirit would be in operation at the Sunday morning communion service, with prophecy alongside tongues and interpretation. That morning, a message in tongues was given and a lady called Miss Ellen Guest stood to give the interpretation. She was Judith's aunt and a founder member of that church. She carried an authority when she ministered in the gifts of the Spirit, so I always paid close attention when she spoke, even as a 15 year old.

'The TWO things you have asked of the Lord, He will grant. He has seen the desires of your heart for BOTH of these things and it will be His delight to grant them...... ' And on she went. Over and over again, she stressed that the TWO things for which I had been praying would be granted.

I knew it was for me.

I didn't have to claim it by faith.

I experienced an overwhelming sense of God breaking through into my time dimension, into my young life and speaking words that could only have come from Him. It was awesome in the truest sense of the word. I was utterly amazed

18

that God was just as interested in my desire to go out with Miss Brookes as He was in me wanting to serve Him. Little did I realize that those two things were complementary. God would bring us together but as well as soul-mates we would be work-mates as we served God together at the Church at Junction 10. In fact, without her, I could never have done the job.

I have had just one wife. Jacob had two. For the next fourteen years, God blesses him and he becomes very rich, with huge herds of sheep, cattle, donkeys and camels. Uncle Laban is becoming increasingly jealous of his nephew's success. His attitude towards him hardens so God tells Jacob to run away. It's time for Jacob to vanish again.

I love the story about a dinner party, at which the host's two children entered the room totally naked and walked slowly around the dining table. The parents were so embarrassed that they pretended nothing was happening – not always a good way to avoid difficult situations – but they just kept the conversation going. The guests co-operated and continued talking but were amazed at the children's behaviour.

After going all the way around the table, the children left. As they disappeared from sight, there was a moment of total silence from the guests, during which one child was heard to say to the other, 'You see, it IS vanishing cream!'

It was time - once more - for Jacob to vanish.

> Genesis 31:17, *"Then Jacob put his children and wives on camels, and he drove all his livestock ahead of him, along with all the goods he had accumulated in Paddan Aram, to go to his father Isaac in the land of Canaan".*

Once more, Jacob is running away but this time it's not brother Esau who is the fear factor but father-in-law Laban. With wives and children riding on camels, Jacob is on foot driving all his herds along in front of him.

Eventually the problem with both his brother and his uncle gets resolved and Jacob goes back home to Canaan.

In Canaan, Jacob was known as a Hebrew. He enjoyed the itinerant lifestyle of a traveller, slowly moving from place to place with his herds. Now immensely wealthy, Jacob is the head of a very large tribe, with ten sons who have large families. His eleventh son has been missing for many years, while the twelfth one is still a youngster.

No more running away for Jacob now. He is settled, well off, well spoken of and well adapted to his surroundings.

Chapter 3

Your Car Awaits!

Hindsight, they say, is a very precise science. Foresight is far less precise. Jacob had no idea that he was going to have to run away for a third time.

The fear factor this time wasn't an angry brother or an irate father-in-law but famine. Fear of starvation now gripped Jacob. He felt it in the pit of his stomach in more ways than one. A famine hit the area where he was living and the whole of the then known world was affected. People were starving to death but Jacob had always been resourceful.

> Genesis 42:1, *"When Jacob learned that there was grain in Egypt, he said to his sons, 'I have heard that there is grain in Egypt. Go down there and buy some for us, so that we may live and not die'".*

Obeying their father, off go his sons to Egypt only to meet their younger brother Joseph, who is now second only to the Pharaoh. The story is well known but if not to you, please read it because it's an amazing adventure. The upshot is that Joseph sends for his father, Jacob, to go and live in Egypt. In order to escape the famine, to live and not die, Jacob has to run again. People talk about 'third time lucky' and this is Jacob's third time running away but 'luck' does not come into the equation. He is about to experience the blessing of God in an unprecedented way, which would far exceed good fortune.

As he escapes from the famine in Canaan, he doesn't 'leg it'. He's not running - or even walking. This time is to be so utterly different. The 'wheels' featured in the Bible for the first time are coming for Jacob.

His third escape is about to be made as an honoured passenger in one of Pharaoh's royal carts. It doesn't get much better than that!

I have no idea how many carts were needed but it would have been a huge convoy because all his sons and daughters and in-laws and grandchildren and servants and possessions were in the wagons. Everything and everyone connected with Jacob was transported. Genesis 46:5 gives us the picture -

"Then Jacob left Beersheba, and Israel's sons took their father Jacob and their children and their wives in the carts that Pharaoh had sent to transport him. They also took with them their livestock and the possessions they had acquired in Canaan and Jacob and all his offspring went to Egypt. He took with him to Egypt his sons and grandsons and his daughters and granddaughters— all his offspring".

Remember carts were uncommon at this time so this would have been a huge talking point amongst the Canaanites. Everyone was out of their tents and houses, watching this massive procession of wagons, people, cattle and Egyptian helpers.

'I never knew this Jacob had connections with the Pharaoh. They say his son – you know the one he thought was dead – well, they say that he is big in Egypt. Have you ever seen such a convoy of carts? I wish I was going with them away from this famine'.

And so the excited chatter of the watching crowd continued. This event would be talked about for generations to come by the Canaanites who witnessed it - and also by Jacob's family.

I was with Jacob as I read these verses, in the cart with him. Filling the air was the noise of the oxen lowing, cart wheels creaking, children crying at the sight of these strange contraptions and the excited voices of the adult passengers, many of whom had never seen a wagon in their life. Lots of shouting ensued as the kids got on board, joined by the raised voices of the watching Canaanites and Egyptians as the wagon drivers tried to organize their passengers and loads. I was there with Jacob listening to it all. But above all the noise and excited voices, this isn't just the start of a long journey to escape famine.

Something royal is taking place here.

Above the excitement and the adrenalin rush of a new experience, this event is regal. It has a sense of majesty about it. This is more than just a convoy setting out for Egypt to a new life. In the air, above all the clatter and clamour, is an almost tangible sense of a royal occasion – not because the carts belong to the King of Egypt – but because the King of Heaven has organized this trip for one of his favoured sons.

Jacob may have lived a very suspect life but God loved him.

Newspapers carry pictures of the lottery winners, collected in a stretch limo, taken to a top hotel and feted like royalty. Multiply that a few times and you begin to get the sense of what's happening to Jacob. For a man whose life has been punctuated by having to run away, being sent for is a radical change. God had moved the powerful man on earth — the Egyptian Pharaoh - to send for Jacob. He is now truly 'in the cart', but not in trouble this time, it's for his salvation.

Chapter 4

The Wagons Are Coming!

You, Me and Jacob ....

Me.
I lay awake, unable to sleep. The picture of Jacob in the cart would not go away. God sending wagons for Jacob after a lifetime of running was the thought that filled my mind. I sensed so powerfully that the Lord had things to teach me from this incident, so I lay still and the lessons began to unfold, one after another.

You.
All of us have faced difficulties in life, situations from which we have run - and maybe run away on more than one occasion. Some we caused ourselves, some were just the unfairness of life. Jacob's story, however, teaches us that God can send us deliverance as He 'borrows' wagons to extricate us from difficulties. Whatever form or shape our difficulties may take, the God who loved Jacob also loves us and He can rescue us. Psalm 22:7-8 sums it up wonderfully.

> *"All who see me mock me; they hurl insults,*
> *shaking their heads: "He trusts in the LORD;*
> *let the LORD rescue him. Let him deliver him,*
> *since he delights in him."*

And God smiles and says, 'That is just what I will do! I'll send in the wagons!'

At times, I've borrowed vans that have seen better days to move furniture or to help clear away rubbish for people but God is using only the best to move Jacob. A royal deliverance carried out with style was what Jacob experienced, so why not for us? The convoy of loaded wagons caused people to stare in amazement as God extricated Jacob from all his difficulties.

So lift up your head and look because over the horizon, just coming into view are God's wagons. No more running because God is preparing to carry you.

Me.

When we attempted to buy land at Junction 10 for our first building, we faced unprecedented opposition. Every week the local newspaper carried stories about us, attacking our good name and our motives. They all originated with a local businessman, who wanted to buy the same piece of land that we were trying to buy. He had tried unsuccessfully for years to do a deal with the owner but when he learned that we were keen to buy it, he was very angry.

The seller of the land was the then Earl of Bradford, a local landowner who lived at Weston Park. I negotiated through his land agent by telephone. 'How much are you willing to offer the Earl for the land?' he asked me. As we had no money, just a few people but lots of faith, I calmly replied, 'We can offer £5000'. He coughed politely, obviously taken aback by the paucity of our offer but in my simplicity and naivety, I believed that God would make a way.

The land was 0.9 of an acre, adjacent to one of the busiest motorway junctions in Britain, and ripe for development. It was divided right down the middle by a barbed wire fence, with horses grazing on both sides. 'Which half do you want for your £5,000?' he asked. Looking back, there have been a number of times when I have spoken and, in hindsight, realized that the words came directly from heaven. 'Both sides, please' I heard myself say. 'I'll come back to you when I have consulted with the Earl' was his rather offhand response.

Our offer was accepted. The local businessman was very unhappy to put it mildly. He contacted the Earl with a counter offer. 'Whatever they have offered you, I will pay seven times more!' Even the landed gentry could not refuse such an offer. He was offering £35,000 against our £5,000, which back in

1979 was a considerable difference. For some reason, the Earl refused it. When I asked the land agent why the Earl had accepted a much lower bid from us, he simply said, 'The Earl of Bradford said that he supports what you are doing .... '

I had never met the Earl. I never did meet him. I have no idea how he knew anything about us and our newly planted church. I have no evidence of his attitude towards the gospel. All I do know is that God gave us favour with him.

Jacob.
God did a similar thing for Jacob. The King of Egypt, the Pharaoh, was a heathen dictator but God warmed his heart towards Jacob.

You, Me + Jacob.
The Lord has the most wonderful way of bringing us help and blessing from some most unexpected sources. Remember that these carts which God 'borrowed' were the latest technology of their day and very uncommon. Pharaoh didn't run a rental company for 'top of the range' carts but lent his own. This was an unusual – maybe a unique – happening. Do you know what this story teaches me? 'John – when you are serving Jesus, always expect the unexpected!' It teaches me another lesson too. 'John - don't allow previous difficulties to prevent you from trusting God this time!'

Me.
I wrote and thanked the Earl for his kindness towards us but got no reply. It was my first and only dealing with him and he died soon afterwards but God had warmed his heart towards us.

As I lay thinking on these things, sleep had long since gone and I was now more awake than ever. Still the lessons came.

Pharaoh's carts, rolling over the horizon, were evidence that Joseph was still alive. The son thought to be dead for so long was behind all this. *"Jacob was stunned; he did not believe them. But when ..... he saw the carts Joseph had sent to carry him back, the spirit of Jacob revived"*. The carts were rock solid proof that his beloved son was still alive after all these years of thinking he was dead.

You.
Get ready to receive evidence that the Lord is still on your case. Get ready to receive evidences that the dream is not dead. Coming over your horizon will be 'wagons' which shout that the plan is still in operation and that God has not forgotten His promise. The approaching wagons say *"Be confident of this, that he who began a good work in you will carry it on to completion until the day of Christ Jesus"*. (Phil 1:6). Look for uncommon events. The wagons are coming.

Jacob.
The Bible gives no indication of how long the journey to Egypt took but the end of the journey was the beginning of even more blessing for Jacob. *"So Joseph settled his father and his brothers in Egypt and gave them property in the best part of the land, the district of Rameses, as Pharaoh directed"*. (Gen 47:11)

You and Me.
Life can squeeze us into a mindset which accepts just surviving, just managing, just getting by, when all the time God wants us to expect 'the best'. Jacob loved God with all his heart. The mistakes he made were because he was desperate for God's best. He wanted the birthright, he wanted the blessing and to be part of the family tree that would one day produce the Christ. He was passionate for God and the things of God. In return, God gave him his best and arranged for Egypt, the greatest nation on earth at this time, to also give of its best. The family was settled in the best part of the land.

The Bible speaks of abundance, of overflowing, of *"good measure, shaken together and running over"*. It promises so much blessing that it cannot be contained. Jesus arranged for his disciples to land a catch of fish so huge that it broke the nets. Peter in his letter writes of *"an inexpressible joy"*. Our God is into more than just meeting needs. He is the God of the 'much more'.

Three times Jacob has had to run.

Such repeated life experiences can cause a person to begin to believe that life will always be the same. It will always be difficult. It will always put us on the back foot. Our mindset gets shaped into expecting failure and restriction and poverty. This is the way it has always been so why should it change now?

It can change because there are times when God sends in royal wagons. Why not begin to expect some of God's best? Why tie God's hands with unbelief? 'Here we go again' Jacob could so easily have thought but it was different this time. The wagons were coming. Satan is a master at lulling us into 'always making do' with second best but our God has different plans. God sent the royal fleet of wagons for Jacob and his kids. Peter says that we are a royal priesthood so lift your head and look up. The best is yet to be because the wagons are coming!

Me.
I rolled over and looked at the clock. It was 2.30am but still new thoughts tumbled through my mind about Jacob and the wagons.

Riding on Dolly's back did something for me as a kid. I felt so grown up, even though I wasn't even controlling the horse.

Jacob.
Riding in Pharaoh's royal carts did something for Jacob too. Joseph takes his dad to meet his boss, the Pharaoh. *"Joseph brought his father Jacob in and presented him before*

Pharaoh. And Jacob blessed Pharaoh.... " (Gen 47:7)

I love that! Who is taking precedence here? Jacob blessed the most powerful man on earth because he was one of God's chosen. It was Jacob who blessed the Pharaoh and not the other way round. Two verses later, he blesses him again and then goes out from his presence. There is one man in the driving seat here and it is not Pharaoh.

I suspect that if Jacob had had to run away from the famine as he did from his others problems – on foot - he wouldn't have made it. Age had caught up with him but God arranged to borrow the wagons to carry him and now Jacob is blessing the one who owned them.

You.
All this reminds me forcibly of Deuteronomy 28:13.

> *"And the LORD will make you the head and*
> *not the tail; you shall be above only, and not*
> *be beneath, if you heed the commandments*
> *of the LORD your God, which I command*
> *you today, and are careful to observe them".*

Obedience to the Lord will put you in the driving seat of any situation. Remember who you are – a son, a daughter of the Almighty. When God sent the wagons for Jacob they took him into exalted company, right into the palace of the greatest ruler of his day. God turned a disaster—a famine — into a triumph as Jacob mixes with royalty. It is important that we don't allow the crises of life to give us spiritual amnesia. You deserve the best - not because of what you've done either good or bad - but simply because of who you are. So, God's child, take a look over the horizon because the wagons are coming!

Jacob, You and Me.
There was to be one final thought before I finally fell asleep, probably the most wonderful of all the 'cart' blessings. Joseph

sent Pharaoh's carts for Jacob but the whole family were transported in them.

> Gen 46:5, "*Then Jacob left Beersheba, and Israel's sons took their father Jacob and their children and their wives in the carts that Pharaoh had sent to transport him ....* "

The verse clearly states that Pharaoh had sent the carts for Jacob - "*to transport him*" - but his sons are in the carts too. We need to pause at this point and grasp the significance of what we have just read. Jacob's sons are with him in the royal wagons but there is no way they deserved to be. If you were riding on public transport you would probably be advised to get off if these men got on. These brothers of Joseph didn't deserve to be sitting next to their father, travelling in style, in the finest wheeled transport of the day. They were terrible men as a look at some of their activities proves.

- As a group, they sold Joseph, their youngest brother into slavery into Egypt and then lied to their father about it.

- The brothers Simeon and Levi murdered every man in the city of Shechem because one of them had raped their sister, Dinah. When every male in the city was dead the rest of them came and looted the city. They took everything, including the murdered men's women and children.

- Reuben was Jacob's firstborn but he slept with his father's concubine, Bilah. She was the mother of some of Reuben's younger half brothers.

- Judah was Jacob's fourth son by Leah and his name means "praise". Probably the 'best of the bunch', he still gets tricked into sleeping with his daughter-in-law and she produces twins from that liaison.

Do you get the picture of what a family this was like? Imagine having this family as neighbours – they would be the ultimate neighbours from hell. But no matter, they all travelled in the royal wagons to Egypt.

Why? Because of Jacob!

God will bless your family because of you. No matter how dysfunctional or ungodly, they will get some of the overspill of God's blessing upon you.

In the ancient world, the extended family included the man and his wife or wives. These were concurrent wives as they practiced polygamy. He also could have concubines (probably not too many of us have those). There were female slaves (for some 21st century men, this is translated 'wife'). His sons and unmarried daughters and daughters-in-law were included as were his grandchildren, aged parents and grandparents.

Others living in the same home and considered as part of the family were his servants and their children, aliens or strangers who attached themselves to the family for a time. This was the extended family.

Imagine doing the weekly 'shop' for a family this size? I remember once wheeling a trolley around our local supermarket when the kids were young. At one point, all I had in the trolley were several cans of baked beans, several cans of cat food and a box of herbs. There were many other items on my list but that was all I had so far bought. Two ladies walked past me, looked into my trolley and started making comments. I looked straight at them, smiled and said, 'The kids love it! Heat the baked beans, warm up the cat food and mix in the herbs. They'll never know!' A look of horror crept over the faces of the two women as I walked away. My kids didn't look too pleased either!

You and Me.

Extended families were large but as part of it, each member had one person designated as their kinsman-redeemer. That is an old word and old concept but age doesn't rob it of its wonder. The duties of the kinsman-redeemer are clearly laid out in the Bible but I just want to say this — whenever a family member was in trouble, the kinsman-redeemer helped out.

The kinsman-redeemer is a wonderful picture of Jesus.

In 21st century, we Christians are to fulfill that role in our natural families.

We are to bless them, help them, share what God has given us with them. We should be the first person they call when they are in trouble and because they are family, they should be in the wagons with us.

I have listened to so many stories of Christians who are the 'kinsman-redeemer' for their wider family. They would never use that term but they fulfill the role — helping out, sorting problems, giving love and advice and care, just being there in times of crisis. Some denominations and churches have taught that Christians should cut themselves off from other members of their family who are not followers of Jesus. That is alien to everything I read in Scripture. I believe that God wants to bless our family because of us. He wants them to get some of the overspill of his anointing upon you.

Chapter 5

What Did You Say?

It was as I stood in the bathroom, toothbrush in right hand, toothpaste in the left, preparing to clean my teeth that I noticed it. It took my breath away. To save money in these time of financial stringency, we bought some very expensive toothpaste that offered 'Buy one, get one free'. Just about to use tube no. 1 for the first time, I saw the instructions – 'Squeeze from bottom: Push towards cap'. I stood transfixed by the inanity of it and a spirit of grumpiness rose within me as I began to talk to myself. 'What kind of nanny society are we living in when we have to be told how to use a tube of toothpaste? I've been squeezing tubes of toothpaste for sixty years. Who on earth had the bright idea to put this instruction of this tube?' (This kind of reaction can occur when you reach the maturity of your sixties and may re-occur as we travel together but I will try to keep it to a minimum).

I have no intention of insulting your intelligence as the toothpaste manufacturer did mine. I am sure that you have fully grasped all that I shared in the last chapter but I do want to summarize as we conclude this first section. It was almost morning when I finally fell asleep but I sensed I'd heard something from the Lord that I want make certain you hear too.

I believe that the carts or wagons represent God's abundant blessing towards you. Luke 6:36 is a favourite Scripture of mine.

> *"Give and it will be given to you. A good measure, pressed down. shaken together and running over, will be poured into your lap. For with the measure you use, it will be measured to you."*

As you give yourself unreservedly to God, to the work of God, to your extended family, to other people, then a 'shaken together and running over' blessing is God's promise to you.

He will send in the wagons, containing -
uncommon blessing.
undeserved blessing.
unexpected blessing.
unlimited blessing.

There were sixty six other people blessed because of God's favour towards Jacob. Look to be a life source for others as you allow the life of God to flow into you and then out again to those around you.

The Living Bible puts Genesis 45:27 like this:

"When (Jacob) saw the wagons filled with food that Joseph had sent him, his spirit revived"

It's time for revival.

Your spirit to be revived.
Your hope to be restored.
Your joy to be inexpressible.
Your trust in God to be strengthened.

Why?

Because the wagons are coming!

POST SCRIPT

Our book title is 'GOD'S Wheels'. These aren't, are they? Surely they belonged to Pharaoh? Good question.

The fleet of wagons that Joseph brought to carry Jacob and his family into Egypt did belong to the King of Egypt but – for a time - the King of Heaven borrowed them. For the period of time during the journey from Canaan to Rameses in Egypt, they were God's wheels and then they were handed back.

As you read through the Bible you find that the Maker of all things is, at times, also a borrower. He borrowed all kinds of things. For example, from Peter he borrowed a boat to use as a pulpit, from a member of his audience he borrowed a coin to use as a preaching aid and from a boy he borrowed his lunch. On arrival to our earth, he borrowed a manger and as he prepared to leave he borrowed a tomb.

The Pharaoh found himself lending his wagons to the Lord. There's a verse in Proverbs 22:7 which says, *"The borrower is servant to the lender"* but that wasn't so in this case. God never became the King of Egypt's servant but there is a special blessing in lending to the Lord. Why not seriously consider lending what you have to the Lord? Why not give back to Him your car or van or MPV?

There are many times when other people would greatly benefit from a lift to church or hospital or on holiday or to the shops. A dear friend of mine always seems to get a great deal when he changes his car. He is always 'lending his car' to the Lord in one way or another, to help this or that person. I wonder whether the Lord is so grateful for the repeated loan that He ensures my friend gets blessed when he needs to change?

Think about it?

YOUR wheels could become GOD'S wheels!

Section 2

The Twelve

Chapter 6

Car Sick

As explained in the preface, although my love for God has always taken first place, it has gone hand-in-hand with my love for cars. When we first planted the church, I was employed as a Sales Director of small company selling office machines and the very first office computers. My company car was due for change and I was using all my 'selling skills' to persuade the Managing Director to buy me the latest Rover V8. He was somewhat reluctant as it was right at the top of our budget, very thirsty and very fast but I persisted.

One Monday morning he called me into his office. Standing looking out of the window, he asked, 'How would you like that?' He was pointing to his own two year old Daimler Sovereign V6, which was the luxury version of the Jaguar XJ6. I thought he was joking but he was serious. Open mouthed, I agreed. It was fabulous. On a couple of previous occasions, to take out the special lady in my life, I had borrowed it - but now it was mine. Unfortunately, it caused a few problems.

Mark, our son, 'christened' the Daimler on his first journey by being sick all over the rear seats. It did tend to 'float' a little like being in a boat, producing car sickness in my six year old son. But his car sickness was nothing like my sinking feeling when I was taken on one side by an older pastor in my town. Our church denomination had sponsored our first church crusade to plant the church and were very supportive of our efforts, so I was taken aback when my older colleague said to me, 'You'll have no success at all in planting a church while you drive a car like that!' He was pointing at the Daimler. 'It's not mine' I explained somewhat defensively, 'it's a company car!' He shook his head gravely. 'Doesn't matter, the people won't come if you turn up in a car like that!'

Car sick.

Being somewhat hot-tempered in my younger days (and maybe still having to work at it), I turned away and bit my tongue hard but the car business was making me as sick as my son. I could not understand my older colleague's thinking and felt very discouraged. At the same time, I was more determined than ever to succeed. None of the people who began to attend our little church, based in a local school, ever mentioned what I drove so it seemed his concerns were unfounded. (Years later, my older colleague became one of my biggest supporters and friend)

I think my MD got it right when he gave me the Daimler. It was a much better car than the Rover V8 I had wanted and it made the 20 mile round trip to get to church more pleasurable. All these memories came back to me as I read Numbers 7:1-3 on my journey through the Bible, seeing how God used car(t)s.

This Section is about twelve men – not Managing Directors of companies - but tribal leaders, hugely important and influential in their community. They are about to do something unique in the whole of Scripture. Rather than get transportation for one of their workers, they are about to get transportation for their God.

If you were asked to give a gift to God, what would you get?

The twelve purchased six carts!

> *"When Moses finished setting up the tabernacle,*
> *he anointed it and consecrated it and all its*
> *furnishings. He also anointed and consecrated the*
> *altar and all its utensils. Then the leaders of Israel,*
> *the heads of families who were the tribal leaders*
> *in charge of those who were counted, made offerings.*
> *They brought as their gifts before the LORD six covered*
> *carts (or wagons) and twelve oxen - an ox from each*
> *leader and a cart from every two. These they*
> *presented before the tabernacle".*

What amazing verses!

I clearly remember buying both my son and my daughter their first car. Mark was delighted with his white Fiat Panda but Anna was somewhat surprised when her first Ford Fiesta turned out to be brown. 'Black', said the farmer out in the wilds of Worcestershire when I phoned to enquire about it and asked the colour. He was obviously colour-blind because it was definitely brown. It wasn't the kind of image statement that a 17 year old girl would wish to make but it turned to be a great little car. Fathers buying 'wheels' for their kids, husbands buying 'wheels' for their wives or even churches buying 'wheels' for their ministers, I can understand - but 'wheels' for God! Unless I had read Numbers 7 I would never have believed that a suitable gift for God could be six carts.

I have an older sister who buys 'strange' presents. She once bought me a doll which seems a little odd but it becomes an even stranger choice when you realize that I was 47 years old at the time. When quizzed as to its suitability she explained, 'It's a John doll! I knew you'd like it!'

I'm not sure where buying six carts for the Almighty comes on the 'Strange Gifts Scale' but it has to be towards the top. No-one else had ever done such a thing before but whoever these men were, I have an affinity with them. What do you get for the person who <u>has</u> everything – in fact, for the person who <u>made</u> everything? You get Him six sets of wheels.

'Good choice, lads, getting God six wagons!'

Market Surveys will tell you all you need to know about the people who purchase cars, which dealership supplies them and the reasons given for that particular person buying that particular car. However, no such survey exists for this period in time in Numbers 7 but I still want to know -

Who are these men purchasing carts for the Lord?

Which cart dealer supplied them?

Why 'pool together' instead of each buying individual gifts?

Was God pleased with their very 'down-to-earth' gift?

Why carts?

In the next chapter we will try to answer these questions.

Chapter 7

Logistics, Logic and Love

'Logistics' – the transport, housing and feeding of troops; organization of any project.

As a new church 'plant', we had no church building so we entered the world of 'logistics'. Looking at the dictionary definition above, we weren't involved in 'the feeding of troops' but we did have to transport the people who came with us to plant the church. I drove a Peugeot 504 Familiale, with 3 rows of seats and it was wonderful transport.

One winter was particularly cold and we awoke one Sunday morning to heavy snow. 'Not going' was never an option and so with the car loaded with 8 passengers, off we set. The roads were snow-covered and dangerous but we persevered. On rounding one bend, we saw that the gritting lorry was stuck in deep snow. Stopping was not an option either and so we drove past the stranded vehicle, waving as we did so. We made it for the morning service.

During our first three years, we were 'housed' in a local school and took with us what we needed. The hymn books were brought in a box. The banner announcing we were in the school holding services was furled up and transported in the back of my car. We chained the second banner to the iron railings at the school entrance because the first one was stolen.

Sick again!

For our music, two people had to wheel an old upright piano from a small classroom, along the corridor, to the school hall where we met. This caused another bout of that sick feeling in my stomach when I looked along the highly polished wooden block floor because the piano castors had made deep grooves in the floor.

Both sets of parents had chosen to come with us to help plant the church and they were invaluable. The new people who began attending just loved them. My father-in-law, Bill, came up with the solution to the deep grooves being cut into the floor. With the school head's permission we fitted the piano with large, freely running 'whizz' wheels, making it so easy to move and no more grooves in the floor. Unfortunately, there was a downside to our solution. As Judith tried to play it, it rolled about so freely that she couldn't keep up with it so we had to design anchors.

Music was such an important part in those early days.

This special woman who God gave me as my partner is one of the best worship leaders with whom I have worked. In those early days, they were called pianists but she was far more than that. Having graduated from the Birmingham School of Music, she had all the musical expertise necessary - but God also taught her. She had an anointing from the Holy Spirit that lifted the few people in that school assembly hall into the presence of God. That same anointing and gifting was to enable her to train our own musicians, lead our choir, form our worship teams and bring such blessing to the hearers. Our little church became known as the place for Spirit-filled music and sound Bible preaching.

But we were the church on the move – literally. Everything had to be transported, just like the tabernacle in the wilderness.

Moses had closely followed the Lord's instructions and prepared all the fabric, furnishings, utensils and equipment for worship. The finishing of the tabernacle was hailed as an auspicious occasion, with great joy and thankfulness sweeping through the whole population of Israel.

Then the 'twelve' step forward.

Twelve surprising men......

Along with the rest of the nation, the twelve leaders would have been greatly blessed by the consecration of the tabernacle. Watching closely as it drew near to completion, they had a surprise for Moses. While he supervised the tabernacle's preparations, the twelve also had been making preparations and now these princes of Israel stepped forward to bring their gift to the Lord.

Paired off, each duo had bought a cart.

Acting individually, each one had also bought an ox.

Hitching two oxen to each cart, they drove their gift for God to the front of the newly consecrated tabernacle. Moses must have rubbed his centurion's eyes in disbelief.

> *"They brought as their gifts before the LORD six covered wagons and twelve oxen-- an ox from each leader and a cart from every two. These they presented before the tabernacle....... "*

In that simple statement, we find huge lessons for 21st century living.

Here is a group of high profile civic leaders acting in concert. No-one was trying to outdo another. One of them must have had the original idea to act together in bringing a gift to God on this special occasion. Maybe they met in his luxuriously furnished tent, as befitted a tribal leader, shared a meal and came up with the idea? Or maybe one of their wives had the idea first and mentioned it to her husband? Many good ideas in church life originate that way, I have found. Whoever had the idea, it was a good one.

When groups of Christ-followers come together, pooling their creative gifts, great things can happen. As followers of Jesus, we are called to live as part of a grace-filled community. Competition is off the agenda and co-operation is on it. Whenever the church begins to become effective, it's almost certainly rooted in people combining their talents and working together for the Lord.

I love the Willow Creek ministry that involves a group of men who love messing about with cars. Pooling their talents, they fix old cars that have been donated by the church members. They then give them to people in the community who can't afford to buy their own. What a superb example of God using wheels supplied by people working in partnership to bless others.

Women, it seems to me, are usually better at working in teams than men as they seem to be less competitive and less restricted by personal pride? They seem to be able to settle their differences more easily than men. As this incident in Numbers 7 is about twelve men, maybe that is why it is so noteworthy? This unusual gift for God came about when twelve men acted in concert. Male Readers - that needs thinking about!

One surprised cart salesman .....

When my son Mark was in his mid-teens, he was diagnosed with cancer. It was a very difficult time for all the family but especially for him. At that time, he was something of a Land Rover fanatic, buying all the magazines, studying all the different models and knowing everything there was to know about these great vehicles. To take his mind off his illness, we used to go visiting Land Rover dealerships, taking test drives, collecting glossy brochures and talking at length to the various salesmen. We must have given several of these noble gentlemen high hopes of making a sale but little did they know that we were just 'time wasters'. In fact, we made so many visits to the local dealerships that we had to widen the geographical circle of garages visited because we were becoming so well known.

I was stunned a few years ago when I again visited one of these dealerships. I think I was filling in time between two appointments. The Sales Manager looked at me and said, 'You used to come in here with your son. He had cancer. How is he these days?' That was nearly 20 years earlier and he still remembered me. We obviously had made some kind of impression on that particular Land Rover salesman.

Now – your imagination needs to be let loose at this point. Reading the Bible needs to be an imaginative exercise, as we put ourselves in the shoes of the various Bible characters. I often encourage the people in our church to 'read between the lines'. Get into the story. Try to feel the emotions of the people being written about. Imagine the impact on the local cart salesmen as twelve of Israel's finest walk into his wagon dealership - if such a thing existed!

These carts didn't drop out of the sky. Someone got them from somewhere and that 'someone' must have negotiated a great deal as they were buying six carts as well as twelve oxen. Imagine the haggling!

In our first chapters, we discovered that almost all wagons or carts came from Egypt as they had the monopoly on making them. This event is taking place in the desert as Israel has left Egypt in what is known as the Exodus. They have destroyed the Pharaoh, seen all the firstborn in the land put to death and then were given quantities of gold and silver just to leave. So how did they get their hands on six Egyptian carts? I don't know. I do know that these men really had to put themselves about to present this magnificent gift to God.

Whatever we offer to the Lord should cost us......
A minister stood up one Sunday morning and announced to the delight of his congregation, 'I have good news. The good news is that we have enough money for our building

programme'. The people were thrilled. 'However, the bad news is that it's still out there in your pockets!'

King David was buying some land on which to build an altar to the Lord. He was offered it at no cost. I love his response in 1 Chron 21:24,

> *"King David replied to Araunah, "No, I insist on paying the full price. I will not take for the LORD what is yours, or sacrifice a burnt offering that costs me nothing."*

How many of us purchase 'wheels' that cost us a great deal of money but give to God gifts that costs us so little? Our gifts to God of our time and talent and service and finance should really cost us or of what real value are they?

Maybe some of these men risked their lives and went back to Egypt to buy these carts? They would most certainly have had to go undercover to do that. How dangerous that would have been? Or maybe they did a deal with some Israeli mechanics to make copies of Egyptian wagons they had previously seen. How difficult – and costly – would that have been? Whatever happened, wherever these wagons were sourced, they didn't drop out of the sky.

By applying our imagination and being aware of the circumstances surrounding this gift, it becomes apparent that twelve men considered their God worth the effort, planning and expense to somehow get hold of something extraordinary for Him. I need to ask myself the same question.

I used all my guile to get my Managing Director to give me a new car. I always work at getting the best deal for whatever I buy. How much effort, planning and expense do I put into what I give to God?

Chapter 8

Do You Like It?

Some people insist you open the present they have bought you while they watch. I hate that! What if it's awful or baffling or so overwhelmingly wonderful that I want to cry? I usually make some excuse and suggest that I will open it later.

God is now faced with such a scenario.

The six carts have been driven to the front of the tabernacle. What will be his response to them? Will He be pleased? Before we answer that question, let me ask another. What about Moses - was he happy with this new transport fleet of wagons from the twelve?

In the modern Western World, we are used to our gifts to God being finance. We give tithes and offerings, in the offering bag, in cash, by cheque or standing order. This is somewhat dull compared to Medieval Britain when the people brought their tithes into barns. Tithe barns were huge purpose-built receptacles to receive crops, fruits, animals, wine, cider and cloth – all gifts to God. Some of these magnificent buildings still exist and are glorious. Let me encourage you to go and visit one - massive barns, with high roofs and huge doors. Part of these people's giving to God was their craftsmanship and skill in fashioning both wood and stone.

Just as most ministers would be 'thrown' if when the offering was announced someone led in a sheep and tethered it to the leg of the communion table, so I think that Moses was a little taken aback by these carts. The strictness of the design instruction Moses had received, to adhere scrupulously to the divine model of the tabernacle, would have made him very fixed in his thinking. He had heard from God and obeyed orders, which is good but it probably led him to doubt whether he was at liberty to accept these 'out of the box' gifts for God without fresh orders. After all, a gift of six wagons and twelve oxen was very different.

In order to bless God and show Him how much He is loved and appreciated, why not come up with some creative thinking of your own? Bring a gift that costs you - not necessarily in terms of money - but costs you in quality time and creative thought.

In trying to assess Moses' reaction to this gift, we can only make assumptions but assumptions based on what we know of leaders. Moses would have been encouraged as well as surprised to see others sharing in this pivotal moment in the life of the nation. The twelve had seen a need for transportation for the new tabernacle and did something about it. Witnessing these princes take the initiative would have been so good for Moses just as it is for leaders in today's church. There is something wonderful about God's people giving time and effort and gifts to the Lord without having to be asked. Moses, I think, would have been delighted but understandably, he checks with the Lord as to whether the gifts are acceptable.

The Lord himself was very pleased with their gift.

Whenever a group of people work together, burying their differences, producing something that costs them in terms of time or effort or money or original thinking, I believe it gives God pleasure. These wagons were very acceptable to God because He instructs Moses to take them. *"The LORD said to Moses, 'Accept these from them"*. Again, it's just my imagination but I can see these men nodding to each other. It's a solemn convocation but I can imagine them smiling together as their remarkable and unique gift receives divine approval.

God is happy, Moses is happy but I have to ask the question, 'Why carts?'

I don't know how much the twelve had been involved in the making of the tabernacle but God himself had clearly drawn up the specification. However, it seems that the setting up of a Transport Department had been left to their own discretion. Yes - the Levites could carry the dismantled tabernacle but how much better it would be to load it onto wagons. The twelve had obviously seen an area where they could make a difference with their giving.

Why not look at what you or your church or your organization does for God and see if it could be improved?

Paul writes to Titus in chapter 1:5 and says,

"For this reason I left you in Crete that you should set in order the things that are lacking."

What is lacking in your community? You might well have the skills to fill that gap, improve that system, get hold of some 'wheels' that will greatly improve what is currently happening.

Someone spotted a gap in what we were doing to advertise our church and its activities, so they purchased a double wheel mobile advertising hoarding. It cost them both in terms of money and time because it had to be collected from the North of England and towed back to our church in the West Midlands. Both sides of the trailer were then covered with information about our church. Someone else then volunteered to drive it around the area so the information displayed on both sides of the trailer could be read. We parked it at B&Q, IKEA, Morrison's and such places, where lots of people were coming and going. Sometimes we were told to 'move on' but not before literally hundreds of people had seen our sign.

God loves people who use their initiative.

In accepting the twelve's gifts, the Lord gave instructions to Moses as to which of the Levite families were to use them.

'2 Carts and 4 oxen to the Gershonites,
4 carts and 8 oxen to the Merarites and Ithamar,
Son of Aaron, as well as being a priest, is to
become Transport Manager...... '

What a great combination of gifting this man Ithamar had - a priest and a transport manager! You may well have skills that God could use which don't appear in any Ephesians 4:11 or 1 Corinthians 12:28 listings but if a group of men could give six carts to God, what could you give?

As we read the rest of this chapter, we discover that although these twelve men acted together in giving the wagons, they also gave their own individual gifts. On Day 1, Nahson brings his gift, Nethanel on Day 2 and so on because working in a team or a group doesn't rob you of your individuality. You are still unique. Working with others is just another way to bless the Lord.

A group of men were sitting in a sauna discussing business when suddenly a mobile phone rings.
'Hi, love, you at the club?'
'Yes, dear'
'Love, you won't believe this but I'm at the sales and there's a fabulous Versace dress for just £600. Can you believe it? I'd like to buy it'.
'Of course, dear, you go ahead!'

'Thank you, sweetheart. I don't want to keep you much longer but on my way over here I passed the Mercedes dealership and saw their new convertible. It's a car to die for, love. I chatted with the salesman and he said they'd let us have it, fully loaded, for £40,000. Isn't that a bargain?'
'O.K., dear, you go ahead'.

'O my, you are just the best husband a girl could hope for. Just one last thing. I got a call this morning from the Browns and they're putting their London apartment on the market. It would be a perfect place to stay when we're in London. They're giving us first option at £800,000. It's a steal, isn't it?' 'Absolutely, dear! We've got the money. Go ahead and make them an offer at £750,000'.

'This is turning into such a great day. Can't wait to see you this evening to celebrate!' 'See you tonight, dear!' The man put down the mobile phone and asks, 'So, whose phone is this?'

"But King David replied to Araunah, "No, I insist on paying the full price. I will not take for the LORD what is yours, or sacrifice a burnt offering that costs me nothing."

So what is 'giving to God' costing you?

POST SCRIPT

These 6 carts really were God's wheels, weren't they? They were given directly to Him as a gift so it's just fine to include them in a book called 'God's Wheels'. That's alright then.

But wait a minute. I've just had another thought. God didn't keep His carts, did he? He didn't hang on to this gift and use them exclusively for Himself. He lent them to the Levites to carry the tabernacle. In a way, therefore, this is the opposite of the last section. There He borrows from Pharaoh, now He is lending to the Levites.

There are many gifts and talents and things that the Lord gives to us but nothing is really ours once we have given ourselves to God. He takes us lock, stock and barrel. Everything is included. However, those gifts and talents and things He then lends back to us to use for the work of His Kingdom.

Remember the Parable of the Talents?

> Matt 25:14: *"The kingdom of heaven will be like*
> *a man going on a journey, who called his servants*
> *and entrusted his property to them. To one he gave*
> *five talents of money, to another two talents,*
> *and to another one talent, each according to*
> *his ability. Then he went on his journey.... "*

God has entrusted you with many things.

Lent you things - so don't get too possessive about them.

Don't get too obsessive about what you have.

Don't hold them too tightly.

Those things, including your wheels, really are all God's.

When He returns from His journey in Matt 25:14, He'll ask you just what you did with those things He loaned to you?

Maybe He'll calculate your mileage to ascertain how much was for Him and Kingdom business and how much purely for you?

Bears thinking about!

New car(t)s

- to buy or not to buy?

(apologies to W. Shakespeare)

Chapter 9

Laughter!

Tony Campolo in his book 'Following Jesus without Embarrassing God' advocates always buying second hand cars or, as the dealers now like to call them - 'pre-owned'. He covers areas such as not buying someone else's trouble, getting a good warranty and not buying one so old that it lacks the recent safety features. Buying pre-owned is certainly one way to avoid losing lots of money on depreciation. Drive a new car off the dealer's forecourt, cruise around the block and return to the dealer and, lo, the car is now worth thousands of pounds less.

For King David, getting a new cart was about to become a major problem. It had nothing to do with depreciation and lack of airbags although it would involve death.

Samuel gives us the Bible's view on new carts. Fascinatingly, chapter 6 in his first Book tells us about a new cart made by the Philistines while chapter 6 in his second Book tells us about a new cart made by King David.

I love laughter.

I have enjoyed life, although it has not always been easy and we have gone through some very dark times. Just now my two grandsons are bringing me untold joy. I have loved life, been blessed with a wonderful wife and two great kids who are now my two best friends, and many, many other friends and colleagues. That enjoyment flowed over into church life, where we just enjoyed the presence of God as we came together in worship and thanksgiving. Our music should always be exciting. We have always striven for excellence in all that we give to the Lord. I loved sending people out from our services excited and blessed and 'set up' to face a new week.

Sixty three times the word 'joy' appears in the New Testament.

Joy is a feature of the Kingdom brought by Jesus. Nothing compares to the 'joy of the Lord'. Peter writes about being *"filled with an inexpressible and glorious joy".* I have an appalling memory and struggle to remember Bible verses (sorry) but that one from Peter is one that I never forget. You get the idea? I believe that our God is into joy and fun and excitement and family blessing.

However – (that's a word that's always makes me pause) – however – (that's a word that says the foregoing may be true BUT) – however much our relationship with our God is all about joy, He is also an awesome, majestic Lord whom I must always reverence. I cannot 'play' with the things of God or treat them lightly. That lesson is taught very powerfully by the incidents that Samuel relates of the two new carts.

Chapter 10

The Philistine's New Cart

In 1 Samuel 6, the Philistines had captured the Ark of the Covenant – Israel's most sacred possession. A word currently often used in our culture is the word 'respect'. Everyone wants respect. No-one wants to be 'dissed' or shown disrespect. Unfortunately, we seem to show less and less respect for people, for righteousness and for the rule of law. Israel treated God and His ways irreverently.

The high priest, Eli, had two sons who were a national disgrace but he seemed unable to bring them into line. Hophni and Phinehas made up their own rules and treated the Temple disrespectfully. They bullied men bringing meat to the tabernacle to hand it over before it was sacrificed. They sexually abused women who assembled at the door of the tabernacle. These women belonged to an institution of holy women of a strictly ascetic order, who had devoted themselves to God - an institution which continued from the age of Moses down to the time of Christ. Anna was one of these women.

Eli's sons' wickedness peaked when they treated the Ark of the Covenant like a lucky charm.

The Ark accompanied them into battle against the Philistines in the hope that it would give them success but Israel was beaten. Hophni and Phinehas were killed and the Ark captured. When Eli heard the news of the Ark's capture and his sons' demise, he fell backwards off his chair, broke his neck and died. Then Phinehas' wife, who was pregnant, heard the news and went into labour. She died in childbirth but gave her newborn son a dreadful name - 'Ichabod'. It certainly would not appear in any 21st century list of most popular names for boys. It means *"the glory has departed from Israel"*. The 'things of God' cannot be treated like playthings.

God deserves respect.

Somehow we have to cultivate a balanced dynamic tension between the joy of the Lord and a holy reverence for His presence. Eli had allowed disrespect to flourish and disaster ensued. Ichabod was born and the glory of God departed. 'Chabod' means the heaviness or weightiness of God's presence and when that goes, life becomes superficial and shallow.

For the Philistines, however, this truly was a red letter day. They had captured their enemy's god and it was in a box. The 'god in a box' went on a kind of tour but not out of celebration. Each city to which it was taken was hit by calamity. Confusion lead to panic and finally fear began to grip the whole nation. After seven months, the Philistines had had enough and took advice from their priests how this 'god in a box' should be taken back to Israel.

"Get a new cart ...." was their answer.

The idea of a new cart didn't bring the Philistines an adrenalin rush. It didn't cause great excitement when they took delivery of it. They were just aware that their enemy's god was angry with them and great reverential fear had settled across the whole nation like a dark cloud. Little did they know that their enemy's 'god' was about to give them a miracle.

Chapter 11

'Low, a cow miracle!'

One morning, Judith and I went walking. The path meandered alongside a flowing stream and we had to climb over several styles. It was a lovely warm day and everything seemed to be just wonderful until in the next field, over the next style, was a herd of bullocks. Judith was adamant. 'I'm not going through there' she informed me. 'Love, it's no problem. They're just cows'. 'Are you sure they're not bulls?' she asked. 'Of course not' I lied, not wishing to retrace our steps. Very reluctantly she climbed the style and we began walking through the herd of about 60 bullocks.

Slowly, they all began to converge on us. Tension was in the air. Fear crept in. We now had 60 bullocks all following us, getting closer and closer. Surprising how big they are when they're standing next to you and not sliced into steaks on the supermarket shelf. 'You go on and get into the next field and I'll keep them back' I suggested, my knightly armour shining brightly in the morning sunlight. I turned, shouted and wielding my trusty sword – aka my map - hit the nearest one on the nostrils. It jumped back and they scattered, for a moment. Then they all returned again, even closer. They were just about a metre behind me.

It was an interesting few minutes but Judith was away. I caught up with her and finally we reached the next style, which turned out to be a 3 metre high gate into a private estate. The choice was stark - climb this huge gate into the Powys Estate or go back through the field of bullocks.

We climbed the gate.

Although it was a warm day and I was sweating for a number of reasons, I sensed coolness from my wife towards me. I was obviously being judged because of my inability to differentiate between bullocks and cows or perhaps it was the fact that I had lied. 'But what' I hear you mutter, 'has this incident got to do with the new cart taking the Ark back to Israel?'

A great deal! God was about to give these unbelieving Philistines a 'cow' miracle.

> *1 Samuel 6:10: "They took two ....cows and hitched them to the cart and penned up their calves. They placed the ark of the LORD on the cart .... Then the cows went straight up towards Beth Shemesh, keeping on the road and lowing all the way; they did not turn to the right or to the left. The rulers of the Philistines followed them as far as the border of Beth Shemesh."*

Towing the cart were two heifers, which had just calved and had never been hitched to a wagon. The Philistines penned up the calves and then pointed the cows in the direction of the Israeli border. Defying all rules of nature, they headed away from their young. Even more remarkable was how these cows progressed. Cows just don't walk in a straight line unless being lead, they just wander all over the place but these *"went straight up to Beth Shemesh"*.

It is also a fact of nature that cows don't lead as Judith and I discovered - they only follow. Billy Crystal and his friends in the film 'City Slickers' have a great time as amateur cowboys taking part in a cattle drive and learning how to push the herd along. Without their efforts, the cattle would just stop and graze. These two heifers, however, broke all the rules of nature as the Ark of the Covenant made its way back home.

This is how Matthew Henry puts it: 'This was a wonderful instance of the power of God over the brute-creatures, and, all things considered, no less than a miracle, that cattle unaccustomed to the yoke should draw so even, so orderly, and still go forward, - that, without any driver, they should go from home, to which all tame creatures have a natural inclination, and from their own calves, to which they had a natural affection, - that, without any director, they should go the straight road to Beth Shemesh, a city eight or ten miles off, never miss the way, never turn aside into the fields to feed themselves, nor turn back home to feed their calves'.

Exactly!

God gives the Philistines a miracle – bending of natural laws – to transport their new cart because they are seeking to put things right with Israel's God.

Just hold that thought for now. We'll come back to it later.

Chapter 12

David's New Cart

We jump forward one whole book – from 1 Samuel 6 to 2 Samuel 6. Some fifty years or so have elapsed since the Philistines brought the Ark back to Israel and it is still in the city where the Philistines left it. Another new cart is about to be made to complete the return journey of the Ark. Will this new cart bring an adrenalin rush? Will it bring great excitement? The answer is 'yes' – initially!

> 2 Sam 6:1: *"David mustered the pick of the troops of Israel—thirty divisions of them. Together with his soldiers, David headed for Baalah to recover the Ark of God, which was called by the Name God-of-the Angel-Armies, who was enthroned over the pair of angels on the Chest".*

They placed the Ark of God on a brand-new oxcart and removed it from Abinadab's house on the hill. Uzzah and Ahio, Abinadab's sons, were driving the new cart loaded with the Ark of God, Ahio in the lead and Uzzah alongside the Chest. David and the whole company of Israel were in the parade, singing at the top of their lungs and playing mandolins, harps, tambourines, castanets, and cymbals".

What a party!

It was a great celebration with great excitement and lots of noise. David had invited a band to accompany their procession. All the top people were there – the King himself and 30,000 invited guests. You just couldn't fault this event for enthusiasm and planning and spectacle. If the rest of the arrangements are anything to go by, then the new cart specially made for this journey would have been superb. It may even have been a copy of the ones the Twelve Leaders gave to Moses all those years back. Knowing how much David loved God, you can be sure that this would have been the finest wagon you could get.

God had given the Philistines a 'cow' miracle with their new cart when they sent the Ark back some fifty years earlier. Is He now going to give the Israelites an even greater miracle as they take it home to the City of David, to Jerusalem?

No!

Over the thirty years we have ministered in Walsall there have been many 'new carts' appearing over the horizon. Church leaders are always on the lookout for new vehicles on which to bring in the blessing of God. Motives are always mixed but underlying it all is a desire to see God glorified and a desire to ensure that their local church doesn't miss out. 'New carts' in this context are methods and movements and models. How can we bring in the glory of God to our church in a new way?

We checked out lots of 'new carts' - read books, visited places where 'things' were happening, listened to speakers explaining just why a new cart was necessary and how it all fitted together. Truth is, we never bought into most of them. The ones that we did like, we usually introduced in a modified version to Junction 10. Maybe we missed out on some great 'new carts' but we also avoided some disasters. David was about to discover that he should never have got a new cart.

The oxen pulling the new cart stumble.

Uzzah reaches out to stop the Ark falling off the cart and God strikes him dead. Imagine the scene? Uzzah slumps lifeless in the road. The whole party and the music died along with him. The invited guests come to an abrupt standstill. David is angry but also afraid. The cart is quickly parked up at the next available house – the house of Obed-Edom – and David goes home as does everyone else. The party is definitely over.

Why?

Why did God do such a thing? Uzzah was only trying to stop the Ark falling off the cart onto the road and maybe getting damaged? It was just a natural reaction. The Philistines, God's enemies, got a miracle but the Israelites, God's chosen people, get a road death.

Why?

The answer is not an easy one but it is simple. God expects more from His children than He does from unbelievers. The standard is so much higher. *"From everyone who has been given much, much will be demanded ....."* says Luke 12:48. God blesses His children in every conceivable way. He gives in abundance. In return, He asks for a higher standard of conduct. God is a holy God and He expects obedience. The joy of the Lord is most definitely our strength but it also has to be balanced with reverential fear.

Uzzah was only trying to stop the Ark falling off the new cart onto the road and maybe getting damaged – but - the Ark should never have been on a cart in the first place – new or old. David had made a huge mistake in getting a new cart to carry it. He had failed to read God's manual on just how the Ark was to be transported.

As we investigated 'new carts' over the years, some were very attractive because we felt it was time for a change as things needed freshening up, to prevent staleness creeping in. What should we do?

Getting a new car has always been an inherent weakness in me, I must confess. I have traded in cars when I could have run them for much longer. Judith would smile knowingly as I came home with yet another car brochure. When asked the reason for the brochures left tellingly around our home, I regularly came up with fresh, innovative, new reasons for getting another car, none of which she believed but she humoured me.

Many years ago, I remember buying one particular new car because it was diesel and had great consumption figures. As I drove it home I knew I had made a big mistake but could not admit it to my beloved. She hated it and told me so when I tentatively broached the subject a couple of months later. What could I do? One weekend, our visiting preacher was the principal of our Bible College. It was a splendid weekend of ministry until he said to me, 'John - I can't believe that you are driving a car like that!' That did it. I had a way out of the dilemma. I visited the local Volvo dealer who offered me a great deal to trade in the unloved new car and acquire a new Volvo. How could my beloved possibly object when, in explaining my reason for the shortest tenure of car ownership in living memory, I was able to tell her that 'our college principal had given me a word!'

(Dear Reader – please do not judge me too harshly because Matthew 7:1 says you shouldn't!)

Fortunately, I was far more careful about getting a 'new cart' for the church.

Unlike David, I did constantly read the manual of how the Ark was to be transported, how the presence of God was to be carried amongst this group of believers. It was a solemn responsibility to get it right, so we chose to treat God's bride with the utmost respect and care. I also discovered that those early Churches in the New Testament were unique. Each one was different in form and function. There was no one method of leading or ministering or evangelizing so a new cart that might be great for the church down the road just wasn't suitable for the Church at Junction 10.

If David had read the manual on 'Ark Transportation', he would have read about the twelve leaders who gave God the six carts covered in our last section. Let me remind you what

Moses did with them.

Numbers 7:6: *"So Moses took the carts and oxen and gave them to the Levites. He gave two carts and four oxen to the Gershonites, as their work required, and he gave four carts and eight oxen to the Merarites, as their work required. They were all under the direction of Ithamar son of Aaron, the priest".*

Maybe David read this far and no further? If so, that would have explained his actions. These were the Levite who transported the tabernacle when it was taken apart for the journey. They used the new carts given by the twelve leaders and they didn't incur God's wrath. If so, no wonder he was angry when Uzzah died but that, of course, is the writer's speculation and I cannot seriously believe that David never read the next verse to get the answer.

Numbers 7:9: *"But Moses did not give any (carts) to the Kohathites, because they were to carry on their shoulders the holy things, for which they were responsible".*

The rest of the tabernacle could be carried on carts by the Gershonites and the Merarites but the 'holy things' had to be carried by the Kohathites. They were all Levites but only the Kohathites could carry the Ark. Note that these were all Levites but each group was entrusted with a different ministry. Please allow me to repeat that last sentence – "Note that these were all Levites but each group was entrusted with a different ministry". How many times have I seen God's people get upset because God entrusted someone else with a different ministry or job to theirs. There is an old hymn that says,

'There's a work for Jesus, ready at your hand.
Tis a task the master just for you has planned.

70

Go where fields are whitened and the labourers few.
There's a work for Jesus none but you can do.'

One way to success in any work for God is to get the round pegs into the round holes and the square pegs into the square holes. I have sat with my grandkids and done this, pushing different shapes into the right shaped hole. It's called 'shape recognition'. Simple stuff really; not always easy in church life but it does bring great success.

Peter gets inquisitive and asks Jesus about John's future ministry. In today's language, we'd say he was nosey. In responding to him, Jesus is very blunt and says, *"What is that to you?"* 'Peter, do your job. John, do your job. Gershonites and Merarites, load up the wagons and move the tabernacle. Kohathites, put your backs in to it and get those holy things on your shoulders'.

Reader - find out what the Lord wants you to do and do it. It's simple enough although simple rarely means easy. The ministry of getting round pegs into round holes and square pegs into square holes will bring great satisfaction to all concerned.

Uzzah might have been a Levite but he was expressly forbidden from touching any holy thing. He was well instructed in the Law and suffered death for his breach of the law. For people of the 21st century, 'the severity of Uzzah's fate may seem to us too great for the nature and degree of the offence but it does not become us to sit in judgment on the dispensations of God. It is apparent that the divine purpose was to inspire awe of His majesty, a submission to His law, and a profound veneration for the symbols and ordinances of His worship'. (Jamieson, Fausset, and Brown Commentary).

Chapter 13

Always Read The Handbook!

I crested the brow of the hill doing about 40mph but had to hit the brakes hard. Everything on the seat beside me flew onto the floor. In the road in front of me, a large bird of prey was taking off but struggled to get airborne because of the rabbit he had in his talons. I was just a matter of a few metres away from him and would have smashed into him if I hadn't braked. To get airborne and get away, he then dropped the rabbit which scurried away.

David failed to obey God's rules for transporting the Ark. A man died. It didn't need a new cart – it needed Kohathites. When we move into the New Testament, seeing God's new covenant, many of the Old Testament rules and regulations no longer apply. We no longer have a Tabernacle because God himself *"dwelt as in a tabernacle or tent"* among with us (John 1:14). As a 21st century Christian, I don't expect to be fatally struck down for disobeying a law for the transportation of a communion table. However – God calls me to live at a higher level than the world around me.

More is expected of me than them.

The drive for life in a new dimension is not legalism but love. Paul tells the Ephesians (1:3) that we are *"blessed with every spiritual blessing in the heavenly places in Christ"*. I want to live 'in heavenly places' but like that bird of prey that just couldn't get airborne – (and would have died but for the rapid reactions of the author) – there is stuff that I have to let go. Dropping the rabbit got the bird into the air. There are relationships and habits and thought processes that you have to 'drop' if you want to get airborne and live in the heavenly places with Christ. God longs for you to know him better.

There were priests and Levites who knew the rules about

carrying the ark. Why didn't they tell David he didn't need a new cart - he just needed Kohathites?

David was almost untouchable.

In the previous chapter he has been made king over Israel and all the tribes pledge their allegiance. Then he conquers Jerusalem. From the time of Joshua until David, the Israelites couldn't dislodge the Jebusites from the city. They had co-habited with the Israelites but David drives them out and makes Jerusalem his capital. He then defeats the Philistines, the nation's long standing enemy.

David was untouchable. Maybe he was also 'un-teachable'?

Maybe the priests and Levites felt too overawed to stop him getting a new cart to carry the Ark? Maybe they thought that David didn't need advice? Maybe HE thought he didn't need advice? Maybe he couldn't be told anything?

- It's a bad day for any Christian when they become un-teachable.

- It's a bad day for any Christian when he or she becomes deaf to advice and help from others.

- It's a bad day when we sink our talons into something that stops us getting airborne so that we almost die.

'Hold the things of this life loosely' is the word from Scripture. Let things go. Drop them. Some people and places and activities will hold you earth bound, no matter how strong you think you are.

An old man was relaxing at his 100th birthday party when a reporter asked him, 'Sir, what is the secret of your long life?' The man considered this for a moment then replied, 'Every day I drink lots of water! It's good for you, young man.' The

reporter replied, 'That's ALL?' The old man smiled. 'That ....
and cancelling my voyage on the Titanic!'

There are some things we need to cancel from our schedules
if we are to get airborne on the thermals of God's presence.
For David, he should have cancelled the new cart. In fact, he
should never have placed the order for it. He should have
known better. He should have listened to others around him
who also knew better.

The Philistines experienced a miracle alongside their new cart
because they were doing their best to remedy a wrong
situation and get the Ark back to Israel.

The Israelites received no miracle because David was acting
in direct contravention to God's express laws on divine
transportation and He expected better of David.

In 1 Samuel 6, a new cart brings a miracle but in 2 Samuel 6 it
brings a road death. The secret is in how we relate to God and
His ways. He wants us to be happy and overwhelmingly
blessed but He also wants our reverential obedience.
Obedience is the key to everything – even when it comes to
getting a new cart.

POST SCRIPT

We're stopping after each section to make sure that each section has a right to be included in a book called 'God's Wheels'. Seems to me that we are correct to include these two carts because they were made exclusively to carry the Ark of the Covenant and the Ark was God's dwelling place with the Israelites, so carts to carry it, carried Him.

I mentioned earlier the short-lived diesel new car that I bought – in fact, it was a green Austin Montego Estate. It did 60mpg so the brochure said, so I handed over my money (the finance company's money, actually). I didn't like it. In fact, I hated it so much that I got rid of it in 6 weeks and bought a Volvo 740 Estate, which I loved.

Neither of these new car(t)s lasted long. In fact, probably less time than the Montego! The Philistine cart was chopped up and burnt. 1 Sam 6:13-15:

> *"Now the people of Beth Shemesh ...... lifted their eyes and saw the ark, and rejoiced to see it. Then the cart came into the field of Joshua of Beth Shemesh, and stood there; a large stone was there. So they split the wood of the cart and offered the cows as a burnt offering to the LORD".*

The new cart made by David for the Lord, to carry the Ark, never gets heard of again. As I drive around the countryside, every now and then I see cars silently rusting away in old barns or sheds. I'm always curious as to why they aren't being used or sold to someone who will use them. I think this cart ended up like that, parked in one of Obed-Edom's barns, gathering dust and slowly rotting away. It carried too much of a stigma to be used again.

Some things are best forgotten.

Some ideas, ventures, projects and programmes should never have been launched but that's alright. Nothing ventured, nothing gained. Just chop it up or park it out of sight. Two of God's carts went that way.

Solomon

- the world's greatest businessman?

Chapter 14

Go Large!

In 1968, Judith and I honeymooned in Israel, staying just outside Jerusalem. A very dear friend, Jean Holder, who served the Lord as a missionary in Jordan and then Israel, hosted us. She took us into the Holy City and showed us places the tour company tourists never got to see. I will never forget our visit to Solomon's stables.

I think a love for 'wheels' is a generational thing? My son has definitely inherited it and I see signs in my grandsons but if anyone built on their father's interest in 'wheels' and took it into another league, it was Solomon. I remember walking into Solomon's stables not too far away from the site of the old Temple and the Dome of the Rock. They were underground and cavernous, absolutely huge. Solomon had 1,400 chariots and 12,000 horses to pull them. It somehow puts those on today's 'rich list' with their fleets of cars somewhat in the shade.

> 1 Kings 10:26, *"Solomon accumulated chariots and horses; he had fourteen hundred chariots and twelve thousand horses, which he kept in the chariot cities and also with him in Jerusalem".*

Skimmed milk is apparently very good for you but 'skimmed' Bible reading most definitely is not. Rather than 'skimming' the words of the Bible, thinking and meditating on them will teach some profitable lessons.

This verse from 1 Kings 10:26 says so much about Solomon.

Auto industry researchers can tell a lot about a person by what they drive; how often they exchange it; whether its petrol or diesel and so on. God himself also read much from what this verse tells us about Solomon.

Until the time of Solomon, war-chariots had not been in use among the Jews, except to a very small extent. When his father David captured a thousand chariots from King Hadadezer, he only kept about fifty of them. We know this because he hamstrung all but 100 of the chariot horses, two per chariot.

> *"David fought Hadadezer king of Zobah – and*
> *captured a thousand of his chariots he hamstrung*
> *all but a hundred of the chariot horses"* 1 Chr 18:3-4

Solomon, however, expands that chariot base from fifty to fourteen hundred. Why such a huge increase?

Almost certainly, he was trying to keep pace with his neighbours, an early case of 'keeping up with the Jones'. He felt that it was necessary for him to put himself on an equal footing with neighbouring powers. 1 Kings 4:26 has more information:

> *"Solomon had forty thousand stalls of horses*
> *for his chariots and twelve thousand horsemen".*

This is a huge leap from 12,000 to 40,000 horses. Many of these would be stalled in the chariot cities and thousands kept in the underground stables in Jerusalem that Judith and I visited with Jean.

BEWARE OF THE HORSES!

40,000 Horses is a huge number but there is an added complication. God had given a direct order concerning horses to the kings of Israel. Under no circumstances were Israelite kings allowed to multiply them.

Under the heading 'Principles Governing Kings', Deuteronomy 17:16 says,

"But (the king) shall not multiply horses for himself, nor cause the people to return to Egypt to multiply horses, for the LORD has said to you, 'You shall not return that way again.'

By acquiring thousands of horses, Solomon is in direct contravention of God's Law. David kept about 100 chariot horses from his defeat of the King of Zobah, obeying to the letter God's command from Deuteronomy 17:6, but his son Solomon is blatantly disobeying God's instructions by acquiring 40,000.

There are things that God permits in moderation but is against excess.

When the church comes together and the gifts of the Holy Spirit are in operation, do it in moderation – two, or at the most, three. Timothy urges the people to be moderate in their praying, without anger or disputes. He recommends dress sense to be moderate, not 'over the top' fashions. He urges deacons not to indulge in too much wine. God's promise is that He will meet all our needs but not fund our extravagant wish list.

'Keep from excess' is a re-occurring theme in Scripture. Solomon missed the lesson. HE WENT LARGE!

One of the 'founding fathers' of our denomination of Assemblies of God in the UK was Donald Gee. He was affectionately known as the 'apostle of balance'. Over the years in Walsall we also have tried to run a 'balanced' church, avoiding excesses but enjoying abundance. 1 Corinthians 14:40 is a great Scripture, although not exciting it carries good advice, *"Everything should be done in a fitting and orderly way".*

- Keep balanced between faith and works.
- Keep balanced between word and worship.

- Keep balanced between young and old.
- Keep balanced between being 'seeker sensitive' and open to the Spirit.
- Keep balanced between faith and good stewardship.
- Keep balanced between the gifts and the fruits of the Spirit
- Keep balanced between free expression and orderly worship.
- Keep balanced ....

Solomon didn't.

The Levites didn't correct David when he built the new cart and neither did the nation correct his son Solomon as he disobeys God's instructions not to build up the Army's Chariot Division. There's not even a hint dropped that he was wrong. Transgressing as ruler and representative of the nation made the sin national – and so was the punishment.

Over the years, God has given great people to work alongside us at Junction 10. Some have come 'for a season' and some came to stay. I remember listening to Pastor Paul Scanlon from Abundant Life Church in Bradford when he said that every pastor is like a bus driver. Some people get onto his bus for just one stop. Some stay for two or three stops and then get off while some stay on until the terminus. Meanwhile, all the pastor can do is to drive the bus in the right direction.

I am so glad for all the good people that got onto our 'bus'. While every person is important in Christ's church, some are strategic as a source of advice, discipline and correction to the church's leaders as well as being a source of encouragement. If any leader ever gets too big to take advice then he or she is in trouble. Conceit is a killer; so are stubbornness and 'unteachability' – my own word but it's self-explanatory.

Unfortunately, Solomon had most of these behavioural disorders. Military history reveals that before Solomon's time the Israelite nation, with no war chariots, was successful in battle. However, after the acquisition of this huge chariot division - to keep pace with those of the surrounding nations – success turned to failure.

I stand at the counter in MacDonald's. The question is asked, 'Do you want to go large?' Large fries instead of medium, large coffee instead of small and double cheese quarter-pounder instead of a single is on offer.

'Going large' isn't always the best course of action.

Dr. Tony Campolo came to my home town of Dudley in the West Midlands. Warming to his subject, I listened as he urged Christians not to 'go large' when it comes to their cars. He was very critical of Christians buying big BMWs and massive Mercedes. On trips to the USA you quickly get a sense of just how large their cars and trucks really are. They are very thirsty gas guzzlers. 'Chelsea tractors' have been getting bad press in the UK and apparently the cool thing to do is to get a Toyota Prius as some Hollywood stars have done, joining the green eco-friendly trend. We all need to take our share in protecting the planet from greenhouse gases and reducing car emissions is one way.

Parked outside the hall as Dr. Campolo spoke was my 17 miles to the gallon Range Rover V8. 'What I drive is my choice' I thought to myself, rather too defensively. (I currently drive a 55 miles to the gallon1.5 diesel Renault!?) The size of your car is a personal thing, of course, but moderation in everything seems to be a good principle. A large family needs a bigger car than a retired couple but going large for largeness sake isn't to be promoted. However (how I love that word!) don't get too legalistic about it – having a 'big car season' isn't punishable except on your wallet.

Most definitely, Solomon should not have 'gone large' when he built up his wheeled army. He completely ignored God's instructions about horses.

And wives!

The instruction in Deuteronomy 17:16 about not having too many horses is followed by an instruction in verse 17 not to have too many wives! Don't 'go large' on the numbers in your harem was also completely ignored by Solomon too. (Men reading this book - don't copy Solomon!)

Chapter 15

The Wheeler Dealer

If I hadn't been a pastor I would have loved to have been a car salesman! Helping people get into the 'wheels of their dreams' seems a satisfying vocation but the Lord had other ideas for me. Solomon had similar ideas because he also became a wheeler dealer. I never realized until I began to research this book that he set up a business importing and exporting chariots. Isn't the Bible just amazing in what it covers? We just need to 'dig' a bit.

Solomon was the CEO of a Chariot Sales Business.

> 1 Kings 10:26 – 29 *"Solomon accumulated chariots and horses; he had1,400 chariots and 12,000 horses, which he kept in the chariot cities and also with him in Jerusalem...........*
>
> *Solomon's horses were imported from Egypt – and from Kue the royal merchants purchased them from Kue. They imported a chariot from Egypt for 600 shekels of silver and a horse for a 150. They also exported them to all the kings of the Hittites and of the Arameans".*

That's the kind of verse which stops me in my tracks!

It excites me because it is so relevant to life in the 21st century.

Dear Reader - involved in commerce, buying and selling, importing and exporting, trading - did you know that King Solomon, the Bible's wisest man and multi-millionaire, was also in business? The Bible never wastes words so this information is recorded for a purpose. We need to investigate a little more, taking a look at Solomon's business from both a financial and an ethical viewpoint and ask questions such as -

Is he trading appropriately for a Jewish King?
Who are his suppliers?
Who are his customers?
Is he trading effectively and profitably?
Should he be doing this and could he be doing better?

Solomon is importing from Egypt – horses and chariots.

A chariot was of no use without well trained horses to pull it. A little like choosing whether to go diesel or petrol and what size engine, a chariot dealer would offer you two or four horses. Most war chariots had two horses for speed while a double two team would be best for transporting heavy loads. The Bible also lists 'extras' such as iron scythes. The Canaanites fitted these to their wheels when they fought against Joshua, giving a whole new meaning to 'road wars'.

This is just an aside but 'car-park wars' rather than 'road wars' have been a source of difficulty over the years at Junction 10. 'Wars' may be a slight exaggeration but our car-park has provided many tests of our people's Jesus likeness. Finding your car window smashed and your belongings stolen by a passing thief can quickly cause blessing also to be lost.

'Park over there, please' shouted by the car park attendants (outside in all weathers to protect the cars) is not always responded to in the most Christian way either. Christian car drivers can be a miserable, awkward lot. Words have been known to be exchanged and some of Solomon's wisdom could have been very useful to our longsuffering car park attendants. However, back to Solomon -

Just as in today's market, imported cars from different parts of the world have their own particular design and manufacturing styles, so with chariots.

It was during the Hyksos invasion, centuries before the Exodus that the idea of using a chariot as a war machine was introduced into Egypt. By the time of Solomon, they had long experience in their manufacture. The Egyptian chariot was distinguished by its lightness of build. It was so reduced in weight that it was possible for a man to carry his chariot on his shoulders without fatigue. Made of wood and leather, it carried just two occupants - the fighting man and his shield-bearer. For royalty, the 'deluxe' versions were ornamented with gold and silver.

Another producer that came later to the market was the Hittites. They produced chariots similar to the Canaanite and Philistine chariot and it was their main weapon of attack. Each one carried three soldiers - one drove, one fought with sword and lance while the third was the shield-bearer. But if you didn't rate the Egyptian, Hittite, Canaanite or Philistine chariot, you could buy Assyrian. Larger and heavier than the Egyptian chariot, it carried three or four occupants. When we read in Nahum's prophecy of "*chariots flashing with steel ... rushing to and fro in the broad ways*" (2:3-4), these are Assyrian chariots got together for the defence of Nineveh.

So Solomon sits in his sales office, studying chariot brochures. He would have to choose between the lightweight two man Egyptian or the three man Hittite 'hunting and shooting' model or the very heavy Hummer-style Assyrian war machine.

He chooses the Egyptian model.

Why? Why not the other models? Is the basis of his decision made on technical grounds or was profit the decider? Digging into Bible Commentaries reveals why he made Egypt his main supplier.

A little boy badly wanted £100. He prayed about it for one week then decided to write to God. When the Post Office received the letter addressed to GOD UK, they decided to send it to the Prime Minister. The PM was so impressed, touched and amused that he instructed his secretary to send the little boy a £5 note. The PM thought it would seem a lot of money to a little boy. The little boy was delighted with the £5 and wrote a thank you note to God.

Dear God,
Thank you so much for sending the money. However, I noticed that for some reason you sent it via No.10 Downing Street and, as usual, they took most of it.

Not wishing to be political in any way but Egypt in Solomon's day seemed to have been similar. The taxes paid to the king of Egypt for chariots exported from Egypt were very high. Just as high fuel tax makes our fuel very expensive, so taxes made Egyptian chariots very expensive to export. However, Solomon was married to the Pharaoh's daughter so he got his father-in-law to waive the taxes, making it possible for him to import them cheaper than his neighbours. This reduction in taxes enabled him to sell them on at a profit, as verse 29 tells us, to the kings of the Hittites and Arameanst but still cheaper than they could buy them direct from Egypt. What a business man!

You have to admire Solomon but this wasn't a one man operation.

Wisely, he had set up a Buying Department. His buyers were called 'royal merchants'. Egypt was his main chariot and horse supplier but he had a secondary supplier of horses. The New International Version calls it 'Kue'. Most commentators agree that Kue is Cilicia, an important province at the Southeast angle of Asia Minor, between the Taurus Mountains and the Mediterranean Sea.

You get the picture – chariots and horses coming up from the south, from his father-in-law's production lines in Egypt but with the option of horses from the north, from Cilicia. These were some of the finest horses bred at that time. Solomon's Trading Company put them together and sold 'chariots plus horses' to the surrounding nations. How sweet was that!

Matthew Henry in his Commentary has a wonderful view on this wheeling and dealing by Solomon. 'This puts an honour upon the trading part of a nation, and sets a tradesman not so much below a gentleman as some place him, that Solomon, one of the greatest men that ever was, thought it no disparagement to him to deal in trade'

This is high praise from Matthew Henry. High praise should come from us too as we review his business because Solomon was trading very effectively and profitably. He didn't manufacture but 'added value' by bringing the components together and selling them on. However, was Solomon trading appropriately? Should a Hebrew king have been doing this?

Chapter 16

The Bottom Line

'It has been said that little things portray
the true character of a man more certainly
than great ones. A casual reader might
see little significance in the king's assembling
horses. However, the Mosaic Law, in anticipation
of the monarchy, particularly forbade the king of
Israel to amass horses from Egypt (Deut 17:16)'.
(The Wycliffe Bible Commentary).

No matter how much leeway we would like to give to such an astute business man, it is difficult to see how this was a legitimate business venture for an Israelite king after reading Deuteronomy 17:16.

Good profits do not create wriggle room for Solomon.

Spin it, point out the bottom line, put a gloss on it all you will – but something is just not right here. Quite plainly, Solomon has cooled in his walk with God, directly influenced by his many wives and he has allied himself with Egypt both socially and economically.

You have to admire Solomon's business acumen. He might well have fired Sir Alan Sugar to even greater heights. He was obviously trading profitably or he wouldn't have continued. His import / export business was such that the writer of the King's Chronicles considers it sufficiently important to include in the text. However, God had implicitly forbidden such a trade in horses with Egypt.

A quick look at his personal video diary would have given some significant clues to how it went so wrong, reasons as to why he disobeys the Lord so openly. In chapter 3, he marries Pharaoh's daughter, which was before he asked and received wisdom as a gift from God. Bad timing! She was a negative influence on his walk with God and opened him up to Egypt. In chapter 6 he builds the temple, which was glorious and took him seven years to complete. What dedication to God's glory, we think until we read the first verse of chapter 7. It informs us that it took him thirteen years to build his own palace, almost twice as long! Bad timing again!

Hollywood has made much of the visit of the Queen of Sheba to Solomon. Reading only the Biblical text and ignoring imaginative film scripts, it does seem to be all downhill for Solomon after her visit. The Queen pays him enormous compliments in1 Kings 10:7-9.

> *"I did not believe these things until I came and*
> *saw with my own eyes. Indeed, not even half*
> *was told me; in wisdom and wealth you have*
> *far exceeded the report I heard. How happy your*
> *men must be! How happy your officials, who*
> *continually stand before you and hear your wisdom!*
>
> *Praise be to the LORD your God, who has delighted*
> *in you and placed you on the throne of Israel. Because*
> *of the Lord's eternal love for Israel, he has made*
> *you king, to maintain justice and righteousness."*

Her visit seems once again to have been bad timing for Solomon because as you read all of chapter 10, you get the picture of a man who believed his own publicity and the Queen of Sheba's compliments.

He really begins to wallow in his wealth.

He manufactures for himself hundreds of shields of pure gold, stunning in their design and display. These wonderful items are for him, not the Lord. He puts them in the Palace of the Forest of Lebanon. Then he has a huge throne made, inlaid with ivory and gold. There were six steps up to it with twelve lions standing on the steps. The Bible states that nothing like it had ever been made for any other kingdom. All his crockery and household articles were made from gold. There's a great verse that says that Solomon wouldn't have anything made from silver in his palace – it was just too cheap!

This man isn't wallowing; he's almost drowning in his wealth.

We are all aware of 'preachers of the gospel' who have made much money from their ministries. They have opulent lifestyles. Their incomes compare favourably with business people, media stars and other wealth creators. You will have your own opinion about such things but we commented earlier about being moderate in our behaviour. There are things that God permits in moderation but is against excess.

'Keep from excess' is a recurring theme in Scripture.

Solomon missed the lesson and 'went large', first with his Chariot Division and now he goes completely 'over the top' with this display of opulence. It was just a small step, therefore, to begin 'wheeler dealing' in horses for his chariot business in direct contravention of Deuteronomy 17:16.

God is a God of success not excess.

Over and over again, Genesis 1 gives us God's reaction to His Project as it grew and developed and expanded. *"And God saw that it was good".* He loves it when things go right, when his purposes are fulfilled, when His people obey Him, when *"all things work together for our good".* Many of the Early Church converts were people of influence, education, wealth and ability. I am certain that the Lord would have rejoiced in the success of Solomon's business dealing - if only it had not been in the wrong commodity.

The 'bottom line' for any Christ follower when evaluating their business is not the amount of profit. The 'bottom line' is hearing the Lord say,

> *"Well done, good and faithful servant! You have been faithful with a few things; I will put you in charge of many things. Come and share your master's happiness!"* (Matt 25:23)

I read many years ago of a very successful businessman who felt he should become a pastor. He was quite successful as a pastor but nothing like as successful as he had been as a businessman. One day he sensed the Lord telling him to hand over his church to a young man and go back into business. As he obeyed God, he was wonderfully prospered and funded his church in many of their community projects. He tithed 10% initially but as his business boomed, he eventually was giving away 90% of his profits to the work of God.

I also know of several successful business men who have become successful pastors, talking their expertise with them into God's business of saving souls. Our job title is not that relevant. What is relevant is that we do what God wants us to do, that our work is not in contravention of God's Laws and that we are generous with whatever God gives us.

Chapter 17

Spinning Plates

For many years as I lead the Church at Junction 10, I also worked in business, first in the computer industry and then in finance. Trying to get the right balance between God's work and my secular job was always a challenge, as was fulfilling my role as a husband and father. It was like spinning plates.

In the early years at Walsall, the church could not provide me with any income. In fact, Judith and I were among the main contributors. I needed to earn money to support my family which is a Biblical principle. Paul makes this point very clearly in 2 Thess 3:10-12.

> *"If a man will not work, he shall not eat. We hear that some among you are idle. They are not busy; they are busybodies. Such people we command and urge in the Lord Jesus Christ to settle down and earn the bread they eat.'*

"Earning the bread" for me meant unsocial hours as I had to work most evenings. As a Financial Advisor, many of my clients were self-employed business people who could only see me at night, so I worked day and night. To her huge credit Judith was utterly supportive in this. Never complaining, she looked after our two children during many hours when, ideally, I should have been there.

Hard work and the blessing of God meant that we prospered spiritually and financially. My income was 'commission only' which meant that if I didn't sell, I didn't earn anything. That kind of contract imposes continual pressure but also offers great flexibility as to work patterns. I could attend meetings, conduct funerals, see people and do all the stuff needed in planting a church as well as "earning bread".

What I found to be truly amazing was that the level of income we needed each month to live, came in. God met that need.

It became 'common knowledge' in the office where I worked what my target income was. Regularly, month-end would be fast approaching and I would be far short of what was needed. One of the girls that processed our business was a fast-living, extrovert character. So often she would say to me very loudly, in front of all the other salesmen, 'Don't worry John. Your God has never let you down yet, has He? The business will come in.' It was such a faith statement from a girl who wasn't a Christian but recognized when something amazing was happening. And she was right! It always did come in!

But November 1981 was the biggest test.

It was the month that we opened our first church building. From acquiring the land at Junction 10 to the opening our first building had been one long, exhausting battle. On acquiring the land, we naively but boldly erected a large notice-board facing the main Wolverhampton/Walsall Road that declared,

'Site of new church for Walsall Evangelistic Centre'.

Instantly all hell broke loose – literally! We had such huge opposition, orchestrated by a few people who hated God, hated us and hated the idea of us being at Junction 10. We were featured in the local free newspapers almost every week as our planning application took its tortuous route through the local council's planning system. It would take another book to chart the whole saga but merely to say that we were most definitely the 'bad guys'.

Good Friday 1981 was a memorable day but not for any Holy Week reason.

My good friend and our architect, Peter Garner and I were due to meet members of the Planning Committee on site so that our application to build could either be finally approved or rejected. A number of protestors were also gathered. They were vitriolic in their condemnation of us and our new church. Things got very nasty. Peter tried to speak to them and said, 'Today is the day that Jesus was crucified 2000 years ago. It seems to me that if he were here you'd do the same again!' One woman snarled back at him. 'We'd crucify him in the middle and you (Pete) and him (me) on either side!'

I had never before experienced such darkness or anger against the Lord Jesus. Peter was visibly shocked. The hatred towards us and the One we represented was tangible. We caught just a glimpse of what were up against in planting a new church. It was a dark, sombre, black Friday but also a doubly 'good' Friday because as a result of that meeting we finally were granted permission to build. We began in the June of 1981 and by November, we were ready to open.

Three days.

There was so much to do to be ready for the opening. I was so busy with the new building that out of the whole month of November, I only had three days left for my secular job. This really was the big test.

Three days in which I had to earn enough money to support my family and pay the bills

turned into three days in which I experienced the smile of God as I earned a month's money in 72 hours

and three days in which I learned all over again that if I look after God's business, He will look after mine!

In fact, He said something similar in Matthew 6,

> *"So do not worry, saying, 'What shall we eat?' or 'What shall we drink?' or 'What shall we wear?'*

*For the pagans run after all these things, and your
heavenly Father knows that you need them. But
seek first his kingdom and his righteousness,
and all these things will be given to you as well".*

In fact, those 'three days' set a pattern. I could trust God to
meet our legitimate financial needs in fewer days than I first
thought. As my colleagues continued to work 7 days a week,
making more and more money, I slowly reduced my hours
while still maintaining what we needed.

But there was more to it than just meeting our needs.

Judith and I sat in the Hofburg Palace in Vienna. Earlier that
day we had visited the stables and watched the famous
Lippenzer stallions perform their breathtaking routines. Now
we were sitting around a table with six other people. There
were many other tables in this huge ballroom, laid out as it
had been for Emperors of the Holy Roman Empire centuries
before. This was my company's Annual Convention for its top
sales people.

We worked our way through many courses of the finest food,
brought to our table by waiters and waitresses dressed as
they did for the Emperor and his guests. We listened to the
orchestra as they played Strauss waltzes and paused while
the world famous Vienna Boys Choir sang for us. Someone
took Judith's hand and she, reluctantly at first, was waltzed
around the dance-floor where the ladies of the heads of state
of all the countries of Europe had once danced.

The cost of those conventions must have been astronomical
but they considered their 'top' sales people worth it. As I sat
there in my dinner jacket, Judith in her long evening gown,
enjoying the finest event that my company could afford, I
smiled to myself. I probably worked far less hours than any of
these other 'top' people but my God made up the difference.
He not only met our need but allowed me to sit at the top

tables in many of these events. *"Seek first ... and all these things .... "*

And there was another bonus.

As the evening progressed, we were able to share our testimony with the lady who sat next to us. We shared our faith with her, told her about the church we had planted and how the Lord had guided us. She was so eager to know more. The Emperor's palace seemed to be the right place to speak about the King of Kings! The year before the Vienna convention, we had been in Montreux and again had shared our testimony with the wife of another colleague. Anna was so taken with what we said that on returning to Walsall, she began to attend our church and is still with us.

From spinning plates to eating from plates in palaces, I have learned that serving the Lord is never boring.

But please remember these lessons from Solomon's business.

- 'Go large' if that is what God is saying; not for the sake of your own ego but to obey and honour God while at all times being wary of excess.

- If you see an opportunity to set up your own business like Solomon, go for it!

- Be the best business person you can be.

- Do it honestly and with integrity – but don't flaunt your success.

The bottom line will not be the amount of profit you make at year end but the Lord's 'Well done!' at life's end.

POST SCRIPT

But how do Solomon's chariots fit into a book on 'God's Wheels'? These are very obviously not God's but King Solomon's.

Buying and selling chariots plus horses was, in fact, Solomon's enterprise. It was his business. He was a commodity trader and his commodity was chariots. To that extent, these were God's wheels because God wants to be involved in the business of every one of his children. Whatever you do – buy and sell, teach, handle accounts, run a home, banking, painting and decorating, operating a press – all those activities are God's because He is with you in them. He wants to prosper you in all that you do.

There's the important principle in 2 Thess 3:10-12 that I quoted earlier:

> *"For even when we were with you, we gave you this rule: 'If a man will not work, he shall not eat.' We hear that some among you are idle. They are not busy; they are busybodies. Such people we command and urge in the Lord Jesus Christ to settle down and earn the bread they eat".*

Work is a good thing.

It is also a God thing.

Paul tells the Thessalonians that people should not be idle but work to earn their daily bread. As I work, I obey the Biblical principle and so can expect God to bless and prosper that work so my enterprise is also God's.

In our first section we saw how God prospered Jacob's enterprise, which was raising sheep and goats. God did a similar thing for his father, Isaac, but this was in agriculture.

Genesis 26:12-13, *"Isaac planted crops in that land and the same year reaped a hundredfold, because the LORD blessed him. The man became rich, and his wealth continued to grow until he became very wealthy"*.

What I am saying is that Jacob's enterprise was also God's because he was obeying the Lord in it. So it was with Isaac. They both prospered. Solomon also did very well for himself and to follow our principle, Solomon's business was God's business, so Solomon's wheels were God's wheels and that's why they are in the book!

Unfortunately for Solomon, although it was a great business idea – and would have been fine for anyone else in Israel – he failed to read the small print in his King Contract that said he could not amass horses from Egypt.

Mr / Mrs / Miss / Ms Business Person – be successful, go large, use all your creative energies to grow your business but don't sail too close to the wind. Don't ignore what God says, either generally or specifically to you. If He says, 'No horses from Egypt' then obey him. Making a lot of money is not necessarily an indicator of God's smile on what you are doing. Just look at Solomon!

Section 5

Elijah

Chapter 18

Burning Rubber and Riding with Angels

Slipping the clutch while accelerating hard makes for a quick get-away, not that I have ever done such a thing, you understand! To a speed junkie it may sound great but it does the environment no good at all and shortens your tyres' life. This kind of burning rubber, however, pales into insignificance when we look at our next example of God's wheels.

These really are burning wheels – I think?

> 2 Kings 2:11, *"As they were walking along and talking together, suddenly a chariot of fire and horses of fire appeared and separated the two of them, and Elijah went up to heaven in a whirlwind"*

To be pedantic, this book is called 'God's Wheels' but I have no idea whether or not a 'chariot of fire' would have wheels. However, if it had horses, then surely it must also have had wheels? To help me with this chariot, I turned to a number of Bible Commentaries.

The first three made no comment but the fourth one said, 'All further questions concerning the nature of the fiery chariot …..are to be set down as useless trifles, which go beyond the bounds of our thought and comprehension'. Not much encouragement there then although I have always enjoyed the other kind of trifles.

However, every other form of transportation pales into insignificance compared to Elijah's chariot of fire.

There has never been transportation like this. What jaw dropping transport God sent for Elijah - a chariot pulled by horses of fire. It appeared to be descending upon them from the clouds or maybe running towards them upon the ground.

This section of 'God's Wheels' will be unlike the rest of the book because this chariot is unlike anything else in the Bible. There will a high percentage of 'maybe's', 'possibly' and 'don't knows'.

Angels

At this time, the souls of all the faithful were carried by an invisible guard of angels into the bosom of Abraham but Elijah doesn't comply with the 'usual'. His soul is still resident in his body when he goes to God, so it needs something different.

The angels coming for Elijah appear in the form of a chariot and horses. It's as if he is riding in state, riding in triumph like a prince or a conqueror. As we have discovered in previous chapters, the chariot was the mightiest weapon then known, so this chariot of fire is symbolic of God's supreme power.

Guardian Angels

What Jesus alludes to in Matthew 18:10 establishes the notion for many that every person has a guardian angel. These mighty beings always have access to God, to receive orders relative to the management of their charge. However, the whole subject of angels is wide and varied.

If you type the word 'angels' into the World Wide Web, it says there are 357 million web sites on the subject. It has taken on New Age connotations, with shops selling all kinds of doll-like representations and items related to angels. Increasingly, people regard them as a kind of lucky charm to ward off evil and keep them safe. Many of the web sites link together angels, aromatherapy, crystals, tarot, incense and sacred spaces.

None of this resonates with what is happening to Elijah.

Chariot Angels

Angels are called in Scripture cherubim and seraphim. 'Seraphim' signifies fiery. God is said to make them a flame of fire (Psalm 104:4). 'Cherubim', many commentators think, signifies chariots!? There are those amazing verses in Psalm 18 about the Almighty.

Psalm 18:9, *"He bowed the heavens also,*
And came down with darkness under His feet.
And He rode upon a cherub, and flew; He flew
Upon the wings of the wind. He made darkness
His secret place; His canopy around Him was dark
waters and thick clouds of the skies. From
the brightness before Him, His thick clouds passed
with hailstones and coals of fire". (NKJV).

God rides upon a cherub!

Dispels the idea of a cherubic smile on a garden gnome-like figurine, doesn't it? Replace that idea with that of a war chariot. Some Bible experts then link these ideas of Elijah's chariot of fire with Ezekiel's vision of four living creatures and wheels, like horses and chariots. Even the secular world seems to have heard about Ezekiel's wheels.

Ezek 1:15, *"As I looked at the living creatures,*
I saw a wheel on the ground beside each creature
with its four faces. This was the appearance and
structure of the wheels They sparkled like chrysolite,
and all four looked alike. Each appeared to be made
like a wheel intersecting a wheel. As they moved, they
would go in any one of the four directions the creatures
faced; the wheels did not turn about as the creatures
went.

Their rims were high and awesome, and all four rims
were full of eyes all around. When the living

creatures moved, the wheels beside them moved; and when the living creatures rose from the ground, the wheels also rose.

Wherever the spirit would go, they would go, and the wheels would rise along with them, because the spirit of the living creatures was in the wheels".

Well, yes, thank you, Ezekiel!

Better authors than I have written paragraphs, chapters and even whole books devoted to Ezekiel's wheels but in the words of Ps 139:6, *"Such knowledge is too wonderful for me, too lofty for me to attain."* I am not going to go there because it's way above my learning and understanding. However, although we call them Ezekiel's wheels, they most definitely are God's wheels - so they're in this book and there is some kind of angelic link between Elijah's chariot of fire and Ezekiel's wheels.

They are both some kind of manifestation of fiery seraphim and chariot cherubim. God is sending his top-of-the-range transport for Elijah; but hold that thought!

Chapter 19

Hot Wheels

Our first chapter dealt with God sending the King of Egypt's royal motorcade for his servant, Jacob. The wagons came. He stopped running – 'legging it' – and rode in style. 'Beat that' could be written across that episode. It was wondrous to behold and amazing to be carried in those carts but God is about to top that transportation.

Moses was unique in his departure because God himself undertook to be his undertaker. His burial was personally supervised by the Lord himself.

Enoch also left this world in a unique way. He walked with God and suddenly 'was not'. He was taken directly into the presence of God without dying.

None of them, however, had a departure quite as dramatic as this one – a chariot of fire!

- So why did God 'take Elijah out' in such a way?

- Why was Elijah's departure in a chariot of fire?

Beginning at 1 Kings 17, I read Elijah's life story, looking for clues. Elijah was opposed to the accepted standards of his day, when belief in many gods was normal. He believed in the ONE God. His role was that of God's instrument of judgment upon a wayward Israel, which was evidenced by their widespread idolatry. A life-or-death struggle was taking place between the religion of Jehovah and Baal worship as Elijah's miraculous ministry took centre stage.

Elijah's views were in conflict with those of King Ahab.

Ahab had attempted to cultivate economic ties with Israel's

neighbours, especially Tyre. One of the consequences was that he had married Jezebel, a daughter of Ethbaal, king of Tyre. Ahab saw no harm in participating in the religion of his neighbours, particularly the religion of his wife, so he established a Baal Worship Centre at Samaria. He was completely under Jezebel's seductive influence when suddenly Elijah appeared on the scene. This was the starting gun for such a tussle between these three. What a battle was to ensue between this king and queen and prophet!

As I read theses chapters some clues began to form in my mind as to why – perhaps - the Lord sent such transport for Elijah? These are only my ideas; you may have your own.

Things come to a head between Elijah and Ahab, between God and the false god Baal, between God's man and the 450 false prophets of this awful religion. In Baal worship, human victims were sacrificed to him in order to appease his anger in time of plague or other trouble. The victim was usually the first-born of the one making the sacrifice and he or she was burnt alive! In the Old Testament this is euphemistically termed *"passing"* the victim *"through the fire"* (2 Kings 16:3; 21:6). The showdown between Elijah and the purveyors of this obscenity of a religion was on Mount Carmel.

You can read this nation-changing story in 1 Kings 18. Elijah, through the Lord's power, wins and destroys the 450 prophets of Baal. However, he is now flowing in a powerful anointing of the Spirit of God and informs Ahab that the drought that has afflicted Israel for 3 years is about to end. Then we read 1 Kings 18:44,

> *"So Elijah said, "Go and tell Ahab, 'Hitch up your chariot and go down before the rain stops you.'" Meanwhile, the sky grew black with clouds, the wind rose, a heavy rain came on and Ahab rode off to Jezreel. The power of the LORD came upon Elijah and, tucking his cloak into his belt, he ran ahead of*

Ahab all the way to Jezreel."

Imagine it!

King Ahab would have the finest chariot money could buy. He was that sort of man and Jezebel encouraged him in it. He jumps into his top-of-the-range set of wheels and sets off for Jezreel to get home before the storm begins. There was no polite offer of a place in his chariot for Elijah. Ahab hated him, feared him with every fibre of his being. He had just witnessed the massacre of his Baal prophets and now this wild man from Tishbeh in the territory of Naphtali is giving him orders to 'get home'. He roars off, wheels spinning, consumed with fury.

Over the year at Junction 10, there arose the rumour that my driving wasn't always saintly! Tales would be told of excessive speed. I can't think how such rumours arose but one day, in one service, I was presented with a fish sticker. My brother-in-law, Andre, one of our church elders, felt I should affix it to the rear of my car. There was much laughter from the congregation, much nodding and winking. I still have the fish sticker, kept safely in my desk drawer awaiting the day when I feel I am worthy to carry such a Christ-like symbol on my vehicle.

(I regularly drive 20,000+ miles per annum. During my rebellious non-fish sticker days, I never had an accident or any points on my licence. Five or more years ago, mpg suddenly became more important than mph. More barbed comments followed as I began driving like a monk! Unbelievably, I then accumulated nine points on my licence for speeding; all of them for doing over 30mph on roads I thought were 40mph! There's a lesson there somewhere which I am still trying to fathom?)

I rarely spin my wheels.

As a pastor, such excessive behaviour doesn't seem 'right' but

I think Ahab probably spun his, out of absolute fury. Elijah watches him as he takes off for Jezreel. Then, calmly tucking his long cloak into his belt to prevent it tripping him up, he begins to run. The weather is foul and heavy rain lashes across the top of Carmel as Elijah sets off. Ahab has a head start on him in his superfast chariot but Elijah has the power of the Lord. I can't think of any other incident where God gave a man power to run but He accelerates Elijah. No man can outrun a chariot but this prophet of God did. Almost immediately he was in front of Ahab because the Bible says that "*he ran AHEAD of Ahab all the way to Jezreel ....* "

From Carmel to Jezreel was about 30 miles. Elijah is running in foul weather, soaked to the skin, hotly pursued by King Ahab. I wonder what thoughts ran through his mind as his body ran through the mud?

It's rare indeed for the Bible to make any comment on people's emotional reaction to situations. Have you noticed that? It states facts and ignores feelings unlike our world which seems to major on emotions and ignore truth. What was Elijah thinking as he pounded out these 30 miles? Thirty miles! That is a long way to run over uneven terrain, in darkness, in appalling weather conditions. Again, just my imagination but I wonder if he was coveting Ahab's wheels? I wonder if he wished God provided prophets with top-of-the-range chariots like Ahab and TV evangelists?

The exact time-line of what happened when he and Ahab reached Jezreel is uncertain but we do know that Ahab went home to his palace and his controlling wife. He whined like a child telling tales.

> 1 Kings 19:1, *"Now Ahab told Jezebel everything Elijah had done and how he had killed all the prophets with the sword"*

What a pathetic excuse for a king this man was. But his wife was a tyrant. She sends Elijah a text message,

"May the gods deal with me, be it ever so severely,
if by this time tomorrow I do not make your life like
that of one of them."

Maybe it was the last straw for Elijah, that 30 mile run from Carmel to Jezreel? The titanic struggle against Baal and his prophets on the mountain would have sapped him and although the power of God came upon him as he ran the 30 miles, surely he would be exhausted in mind and body. He reacts in a way that was alien to him. He runs away.

"Elijah was afraid and ran for his life....... "

He came to Beersheba in Judah, went a day's journey into the desert, sat down under a tree and prayed that he might die.

"I have had enough, LORD," he said. "Take my life;
I am no better than my ancestors."

Doing amazing exploits for the Lord is no guarantee against falling into the depths of despair. It sometimes goes with the territory. Some of God's 'greats' have also fallen morally just after some of their most effective ministry. Elijah recovers and is mightily used by God after this but he is also commanded to anoint his successor - so this is the beginning of the end.

During my 30 years in Walsall, I have had some 'bad' times.

I am naturally optimistic and fairly level-headed but there have been difficult seasons. When my 15 year old son Mark was diagnosed with cancer, Judith and I entered a really tough season. My GP told me that just one in 100,000 teenage boys got that type of Hodgkin's Disease. 'So why my boy, Lord? Why couldn't he be one of the 99,999 teenage boys that DON'T get cancer?'
During these very difficult two years, I remember going into

the office of the finance company where I worked. It was a Monday morning and maybe I was exhausted from the previous day's ministry. Somehow the situation with Mark hit me very hard and I put my head on my desk and wept. One of my colleagues, a good mate but not a Christian, came in and found me like that. After asking me what was wrong, he said, 'I'm glad your boy's got cancer!' I looked at him in total disbelief - then such anger began to rise within me it was almost uncontainable. I stood to my feet, wanting to punch his lights out!

'That's better' he said. 'You see, John, none of us here could cope with our sons getting cancer but you can. Your faith and your God will take you through this. I'm glad it's your boy not mine.' Then he smiled, put his arm round my shoulder and gave me a hug .

Being in the centre of God's will is no guarantee against difficult times!

Chapter 20

Cool Deal

Was it the race against Ahab's chariot that caused Elijah to ask the Lord to take his life?

Was that just too much for him?

Speculation, of course, but it helps with the idea that maybe it was this run against Ahab's chariot that prompted the Lord to send the 'chariot of fire' for him?

How God loves us!
How He watches over us and cares for us!
What a Heavenly Father we have!

Just because the Old Testament saints hadn't received the revelation of the Fatherhood of God doesn't mean it didn't apply to them. I love the words of Jesus when he said, *"If you, then, though you are evil, know how to give good gifts to your children, how much more will your Father in heaven give good gifts .... "* (Matt 7:11)

I delight in giving gifts to my kids and grandkids. I love surprising them, spoiling them. As a father I can imagine some great presents for my children if I had the wherewithal but Ephesians 3:20 talks about *him who is able to do immeasurably more than all we ask or imagine .... "*.

I can imagine the Lord watching Elijah as he pounds through the wind and rain and mud in front of Ahab's top-of-the-range chariot and thinking, 'My son – one day I am going to give you the ride of your life! Ahab wouldn't give you a lift in his chariot but I am going to give you a ride in mine!'

Maybe that is just writer's license but I love the thought.

"As (Elijah and Elisha) were walking along and talking together, suddenly a chariot of fire and horses of fire appeared and separated the two of them, and Elijah went up to heaven in a whirlwind..."

Was the Lord the driver? Was this God riding upon the cherub of Psalm 18:9 as he rides the wind? 'Come on, Elijah' says the Lord, 'I'm taking you home!' Imagination, of course, but very possible as my God can do immeasurably more than even I can imagine.

As we draw the story of Elijah's chariot ride to a conclusion, I want to tell you one last thing. You need to switch off the TV and concentrate for this final thought ......

Elijah went up to heaven in a chariot of fire but also *"in a whirlwind"*. The word in Hebrew is 'suphah', from a root word meaning "sweeping away" and 'se'arah' meaning "tossed about."

Now - in Psalm 77:18 when it says *"Thy thunder was in the heaven"* it literally means, *"in the wheel"*. If we go back to look again at Ezekiel's wheels, Ezekiel 10:13 is translated in the NIV as *"The wheels were called in my hearing, the whirling wheels ......"* Fausset's Bible Dictionary says an ordinary whirlwind moving on its own axis is NOT what is meant in 2 Kings 2:11. Here in the U.K we increasingly see 'twisters' reported on the news and they are even more commonplace overseas. However, according to Bible commentators, these tornados are not the 'whirlwind' of Elijah's story. It is not merely a feature of freakish weather but, in some supernatural way, linked to God's chariot.

On closer examination we discover more than one mention of God's chariot and a whirlwind.

Isaiah 66:15 almost gives us a rerun of Elijah's experience:
"For behold, the LORD will come with fire and with

His chariots, like a whirlwind, to render His anger with fury, and His rebuke with flames of fire".

Jeremiah follows up with something very similar when he writes in chapter 4:13, *"Behold, he shall come up like clouds and his chariots like a whirlwind".*

This is transportation of unimaginable power.

We have writers from thousands of years ago trying to describe divine space travel. Even today's writers, having seen man's exploration of space, would have difficulty in putting into words the 'wheels' that 'took out' Elijah.

I want you to leave this section of 'God's Wheels' knowing that it's almost impossible to fully comprehend the true nature of this 'chariot of fire' and the whirlwind which powered it.

It's beyond our imagination. We're back to the 'useless trifles' to even speculate. But remember Ephesians 3:20? It says that it's beyond imagination just how much God can do - and wants to do - for you.

When my grandsons ask me, 'Granddad will you ....?' I love to say YES! YES! YES!

I serve a God who loves to say 'YES'.

I serve a God who - I think - gave Elijah the ride of his life in his cherubic fiery chariot.

'My son – I am going to give you an unforgettable ride! Ahab wouldn't give you a lift in his chariot but I am going to give you a ride in mine!'

How cool is that, riding in a chariot of fire!

POST SCRIPT

In our PS we examine whether or not these 'wheels' really were God's wheels and hence can justify their place in the book. No question here. Who else has a chariot of fire and 'rides the heavens'! No, we are definitely in line with our theme with this one......

There is a point we should note. There isn't just one of these flaming chariots, the Lord has a fleet of them and not just the one He used to pick up Elijah.

Elisha, Elijah's successor, saw the fleet surrounding him in a protective circle. I love Westerns. I love it when the settlers are under attack and they give the command to 'circle the wagons' for protection. The King of Syria sends a large army of chariots and horses to capture Elisha and when the prophet's servant sees the enemy, he is very afraid.

There then follows that glorious promise which applies to all followers of the Lord, "*Do not fear, for those who are with us are more than those who are with them*". *And Elisha prayed, and said, "LORD, I pray, open his eyes that he may see." Then the LORD opened the eyes of the young man, and he saw. And behold, the mountain was full of horses and chariots of fire all around Elisha......* "

Elisha had seen the one chariot that took Elijah but now he sees a whole fleet of them in a great protective circle around him. What an incredible sight it must have been as God 'circled the wagons' to protect his servant.

How things change.

Someone sent me a card for my 60th birthday. It went something like this: 'For those born before 1950 – 'stud' was something that fastened a collar to a shirt and 'going all the way' meant staying on a double-decker bus to the bus depot.

Pizzas, McDonalds and instant coffee were unheard of. In your day, cigarette smoking was fashionable, 'grass' was mown, 'coke' was kept in the coal shed, a 'joint' was a piece of meat you had on Sundays and 'pot' was something you cooked in...... '

But some things don't change! Whether we were born pre- or post 1950, God still circles the wagons for our protection!

Candace's Chariot-driving Country-crossing Chancellor

Chapter 21

The Ethiopian Eunuch

Several sections ago, I began a journey and invited you to motor along with me. Our journey has wound its way through the pages of the Old Testament, stopping off at some quite unexpected places. We have also stopped off at Junction 10 of the M6 in the West Midlands as I have told the story of 'the Church at Junction 10', which has been inextricably linked to my own.

Now here we are in the New Testament.

Surprisingly, we pass through chapters and whole books that are totally free of carts, chariots and wagons. In fact, there are only two more stops – this one in the Book of Acts and the final one in the Book of Revelation.

Here at the beginning of the 21st century, the advances made in technology since the invention of the motor car just over a century ago, are huge. During a recent visit to France, I visited Mulhous which is twinned with Walsall. The town boasts one of the largest motor museums in Europe and they have examples of some of the earliest motor cars, which, in reality, are simply horse drawn coaches minus the horses plus an engine. They bear no resemblance to what we drive today. One hundred years has revolutionized car design and technology.

However, the 400 years between Old and New Testaments had virtually no impact on the kind of wagons or chariots that we find. Cart technology seems to have stood still.

An Unusual Combination

Isn't it interesting to see how people dress? What wonderful combinations of style and colours some people put together.

It's almost a case of 'anything goes' and that principle seems to apply to our penultimate wheels.

Acts 8:26-29, *"Now an angel of the Lord said to Philip, "Go south to the road-- the desert road— that goes down from Jerusalem to Gaza." So he started out, and on his way he met an Ethiopian eunuch, an important official in charge of all the treasury of Candace, queen of the Ethiopians. This man had gone to Jerusalem to worship and on his way home was sitting in his chariot reading the book of Isaiah the prophet. The Spirit told Philip, "Go to that chariot and stay near it."*

Guesswork comes into play when deciding what this very important civil servant was driving but our guesses are informed. The consensus among Bible commentators is that this was a covered chariot, covered to protect its occupants from the heat of the midday sun and it was probably drawn by oxen. That is a VERY unusual combination because chariots were usually drawn by horses, for their speed, while oxen were better for heavy work and so pulled wagons or carts.

For a time, my son Mark and I loved 'off-roading'.

In his mid-teens, while recovering from cancer, we discovered that this pursuit took his mind off the illness and the radiotherapy treatment. Taking a four-wheeled drive vehicle and driving down lanes, over hills and mountain tracks, was a special treat for him – and me. Over a period of years we had a Land Rover, a Range Rover and a Land Rover Discovery. According to the brochures, there was nowhere that was inaccessible to us. We did, unfortunately, have a number of embarrassing moments.

One day, while visiting Ragley Hall in Warwickshire we decided to show the ladies – wife Judith and daughter Anna - how thrilling 'off-roading' was and what brilliant drivers we were in adverse conditions. We were ambling along a dirt track around the edges of the Ragley Estate, bumping through a few puddles, laughing at the suggestions coming from Judith that she hoped we wouldn't get stuck in this remote place. How silly! Then we stopped – abruptly! The Range Rover had sunk in mud up to its axles. No problem though – we selected low ratio, selected bottom gear and accelerated. Slowly, ever so slowly, we sank even deeper.

Half an hour later, we found a cottage and saw a tractor parked behind it. We mumbled about 'being stuck ... could you pull us out .... sorry, mumble, mumble'. Humility always comes at a cost. Yes, he would come and help us. No, he wouldn't bring the tractor but would use his old Series One Land Rover. 'What sort of car have you got stuck?' was his next question. 'A Range Rover' I mumbled. His eye brows lifted, he said nothing but a look of utter disdain crossed his face. What kind of idiot gets stuck in a Range Rover on a country track? 'Dad' whispered Mark, 'how is he going to pull out a Range Rover with a Series One?' I shook my head, imagining what Judith would say!

I will never forget his recovery tactics. He had a very long tow rope. He started a long way behind us, with the rope tied to the front of our car. Then he accelerated, driving a parallel course to the track we were on. As he flew past us he shouted, 'Accelerate!' I hit the accelerator, there was an almighty jerk and we shot out of our mud-hole. I thanked him profusely and gave him £10. He nodded. I gave Judith a look that said, 'DON'T SAY ANYTHING!' She didn't, just smirked.

I may write another book on places where we have got stuck and got lost. It will be a kind of treatise on how not to 'off-road' but this eunuch must have been an 'off-roading' expert although I don't think that he would have used such terminology.

The journey from Ethiopia to Jerusalem - and back again –

would have been a huge undertaking and a massive challenge. The return leg of the journey featured here led him from Jerusalem to Gaza on the Mediterranean coast, along the Way of the Philistines, down through the Land of Goshen and then straight through the land of Egypt, keeping the Nile and his left. Ethiopia lies directly south of Egypt.

For a journey of that magnitude, mainly off-road and through desert, he used a chariot as it would be slightly more comfortable than a wagon - but then he harnessed oxen to it. For long-distance travel their strength made them a better option than horses. A covered chariot pulled by oxen, not horses, makes sense but it's an unusual combination – although a well-thought out one. That unusual combination begins to give us some insight into the man who is driving this chariot.

Chapter 22

"Get In!"

When Pete phoned to ask if I had an hour or so to spare, explaining why, my answer was an unequivocal 'yes'. He drew up in a TVR sports car (loaned for the weekend) and invited me to climb in. When he pulled away, he left my stomach behind. The acceleration was mind-blowing.

Dave called, asking if I was free. The answer again was in the affirmative. He drew up in his recently acquired Westfield open top sports car and invited me to climb in. He was wearing a leather helmet and goggles. I thought I was travelling with Biggles. It needed great agility but I lowered myself in and off we roared, the wind blowing through my hair. It was so low it felt as if my nether regions were almost scraping the road.

For me 'get in' is an invitation that I've never been able to refuse. To 'get in' and try out a car is one of life's pleasures. I know, I know - how very sad you are thinking but test drives are irresistible opportunities to get behind the wheel. Whenever someone has a new car, I always ask if I can sit in it, holding the steering wheel and casting envious glances at the shiny new interior and smelling the 'newness'.

There are just two characters in this incident from Acts 8 – a government minister (the Ethiopian eunuch) and a church minister (Philip). The second is about to get an invitation from the first to 'get in'. As I read about these 'wheels', it was the driver's invitation that grabbed my attention. These are very important words. Pete and Dave both asked me to 'get in' as did the eunuch to Philip but his motive was very different to that of my friends.

Let Acts 8:29-31 set the scene.

"The Holy Spirit said to Philip, "Go over and walk

along beside the chariot." Philip ran over and heard what he was reading and asked, "Do you understand it?" "Of course not!" the man replied. "How can I when there is no one to instruct me?" And he begged Philip to come up into the chariot and sit with him".

First a quick thumbnail sketch about this remarkable man who is asking Philip to 'get in' to his chariot.......

- He can obviously 'think-outside-the-box' as demonstrated by the combination of chariot plus oxen.

- He's from Ethiopia, one of the great kingdoms of Africa, frequently mentioned in the Bible as "Cush." Lying south of Egypt, on the Nile, it was bounded by Egypt, the Red Sea, regions in the interior of Africa and Libya. Ethiopians frequently served as hired soldiers in the Egyptian army. Known for their black skin, they were tall and very fierce in battle, so it's possible that our man was a tall, black man.

- He's a eunuch. Eunuchs were commonly employed in attendance on the females of the harem but the word is also used to denote any counsellor of state. It is evidently so used here. This high ranking officer of the court could also have been a Jew or a Jewish proselyte. What is known is that Jews were often raised to posts of high honour and distinction in foreign courts, as in the case of Joseph in Egypt and Daniel in Babylon so instead of a tall black man he might have been a short white man. Sorry!

- Our chariot driver served under Candace, the common name of the queens of Ethiopia, just as "Pharaoh" was of the sovereigns of Egypt. He was a top government official, a kind of Chancellor of the Exchequer.

This man's high position meant that his chariot would have

been just as fine as the royal transport wagons Pharaoh instructed Joseph to send for his father, Jacob. However, his invitation to Philip to 'get in' had nothing to do with him flaunting his wealth or position.

> *"The Treasurer of Ethiopia .... had gone to Jerusalem*
> *to worship and was now returning in his chariot*
> *reading aloud from the book of the prophet Isaiah.*
> *Philip asked, "Do you understand it?"*
> *"Of course not!" the man replied. "How can I when there*
> *is no one to instruct me?" And he begged Philip to*
> *come up into the chariot and sit with him".*

The invitation to 'get in' was not to make an impression: it was a confession. 'Hey, I don't understand this – please get in and instruct me!' He'll give Philip a ride in his chariot if Philip will explain the words of Isaiah to him.

'Riding in cars' and 'studying the Bible' aren't synonymous.

Riding in cars is synonymous with making a journey
or having a blast to see how it performs
or enjoying a leisurely drive through the countryside.

Studying the Bible is synonymous with
sitting in a room
quietly
and concentrating hard.

Surprisingly, God puts them together here.

Once again, as we have seen a number of times on our journey, the Bible breaks stereotypes. Here, God uses something that is associated with war or commerce or political power as the location for an 'on the move' Bible study. It's unusual to ride in a chariot while - at the same time - studying the Bible but I really have to get hold of this concept. God is a God of immense variety. He can put the most unlikely things together. He can put the most unlikely people, things, gifts and actions together - with remarkable outcomes.

Over the years at the Church at Junction 10, God did this many times.

THE VINE

In Lower Hall Lane stood a pub that was notorious for drugs, prostitution and violence. It was so bad that it was eventually closed by the brewery that owned it. A number of Christians from across denominational streams then came together – Anglicans, Pentecostals, Methodists, Baptists and House Church. Their vision was that together they buy this old pub. Back in the 1980's that was a very unusual combination!

Different denominations just didn't co-operate back then. Most of them didn't speak to each other. In fact, they didn't even know each other. God, however, put together some very varied people to reach out into our community by buying the Vine pub, which then became a safe haven for young people. For the first period of its new life as a youth drop-in, it was run by Pete and Jenny Christopher. They worked with the many young people who frequented the Vine but also with the working girls who plied their trade on the streets outside. Nights would often see Pete and Jenny at the local A & E Department, accompanying some poor girl who had been beaten up by a client or their pimp. The Christopher family lived 'over the shop' and when help was needed, it was the doorbell of the Vine that these girls rang. What a wonderful job the Christophers did!

When we re-launched 'The Vine' I was chatting to a senior police officer who attended the event. Asking him whether he had ever been there before, he laughed: 'I've been on more drugs raids on this place than I've had hot dinners ....!'

Still today 'The Vine' is thriving.

We run a host of different training and work programmes for hard-to-reach young people. In Kevin Davis we have an exceptionally talented young CEO who has attracted major funding from a wide variety of sources to further its ministry. It is a third sector flagship project that carries huge respect from both local and national government. Kevin was recently invited to 10, Downing Street to meet the Prime Minister. We are about to begin building 'Goldmine', which is a £4m new build to extend the ministry of the Vine Trust. What wonderful things God can do when unlikely people come together!

FIRST BASE

God also linked us up with a local housing association.

There was a homelessness problem amongst young people in Walsall which challenged us to do something. After many false starts and abortive efforts to acquire property to house these youngsters, God brought us into partnership with Caldmore Housing Association.

They had a complex containing 20 flats plus community facilities while we had people with vision. Again, another unusual combination - a local housing association and a local church – but it worked. The project became known as 'First Base'. Under the visionary leadership of another outstanding young man, Steve Clay, we also built Small Street Centre, adjacent to the housing complex. This became our training and educational centre for the young people we housed. Today under the leadership of Stuart Ashmore, Malcolm Jones and Val Hibbert, First Base is thriving and they have just acquired a block containing 21 apartments.

How our God loves to break down stereotypes as to what His church is all about. On the top floor of our Small Street centre is our 'Ebenezer' room, often used by local churches and ministers. First Base really can say, *"Thus far has the Lord helped us!"*

THE NET

At the same time that these projects were coming into existence, another visionary young man called Tim Fellows was bringing together leaders – both young and old – across the Black Country. He had a 'Kingdom' vision to bring all denominations and church streams together, breaking down barriers and mistrust.

After many years of blood, sweat and tears, there are now great friendships among church leaders across the towns of Wolverhampton, Walsall, Dudley and Sandwell. The story of 'The Net' - as this network came to be called - needs to be written but it will feature high spots such as 4,000 Christians at an all-night prayer meeting, praying for the Black Country. That night of prayer began at 8pm with Civic Leaders from all four Boroughs honoured as our guests and thanked for all they do. As instructed by 1Timothy 2:2, we prayed for them and committed them to the Lord.

At the end of that first session, I remember escorting out the Lord Lieutenant for Staffordshire who was very emotional. 'I can't ever remember attending anything like this in my whole life' he said to me, 'how can I thank you all!'

What an amazing combination that was of Christian and secular leaders, heads of schools, police, health authorities, social services and Christians of every denominational hue.

STEPPING STONES

It wasn't just young men that God used.

'Stepping Stones' was a ministry to victims of domestic violence that was the vision of a lady called Cilla Baker. She herself had a very 'interesting' life story and that provoked her

130

to reach out and help others. Many, many women – and some men – were helped.

CAUSEWAY PROSPECTS

Chris Stringer is another lady with vision. She linked up with Causeway Prospects and took us into the generally ignored world of adults who have severe learning difficulties. Her own experiences with her son Michael showed her the great need in this area. She and her team chose to do something about it.

There are other projects that I could mention but space prohibits.

In today's church it is quite obvious that we should be involved in our communities but 20 years ago, it wasn't. 'Church was church' and a 'social gospel' was anathema to many Christians. Slowly but steadily, however, the Lord spoke to me about such polarized positions. As time passed, God's word to me became increasingly clear.

'Take GOD and take GOODNESS into your community ...... they may not want your God but they will receive your goodness. And then they may ask about your God!'

And I watched it happen - this process of 'taking goodness into our community' - as God raised up the people I've mentioned and many others beside. Riding in a chariot and doing a Bible study was unusual for Philip but he did it. Preaching the gospel with works not words was a new concept for us but we did it - and still do.

We really have to get hold of this concept that our God is a God of immense variety and He can bring together the most unlikely things and people and talents and activities - with remarkable outcomes.

Philip was the right man - at the right time - in the right place to meet and share Jesus with the Ethiopian eunuch. He was sent there by the Holy Spirit. The choice of place for his sharing the Gospel with this government minister at first glance would appear to be the wrong place – a jolting, creaking, dust-filled, moving wagon. However, it proved to be the right place because it was there that Candace's Treasurer met Jesus.

Don't close your mind to situations and people and actions that God will put together. They will have a unique quality, a surprise element, even sometimes an apparently coincidental feel but - in reality - they are God-incidents and not coincidences. Just as surely as Philip's Bible study in a moving chariot was a God-incident, you will be confronted with situations God has engineered for your benefit – but also for the benefit of others.

'GET IN' – THE DEFAULT OPTION AND DEBORAH'S SONG

DEFAULT OPTIONS are numerous in the 21st century. Many of the devices we purchase such as mobile phones and computers have factory settings. Unless we choose to change them, the devices default to these settings.

THE DEFAULT OPTION FOR DRIVERS IS ambling down to the supermarket, pottering along to church, popping in to see friends and family, with the occasional trip to the football match or the seaside......... etc ..... etc ...... etc ....

OR YOU CAN CHOOSE TO GO OFF–ROADING!

Having made this choice and got hold of a 4 -X 4, you will almost certainly get stuck, definitely get lost and in all probability scratch and dent your shiny paintwork. But what an adventure! What excitement as the adrenalin pumps around your body!

THE DEFAULT OPTION FOR YOUR CHRISTIAN JOURNEY

can be similarly stereotypical. Attend church when it suits you. Give Jesus the minimum requirements. Only very rarely get involved in God-inspired risk-taking, which is another word for faith. You will then be able to accurately prophesy exactly what you will do for Jesus from now until the day God calls you home - very little!

OR YOU CAN CHOOSE TO GET IN!

With the eye of faith you spot a new opportunity to serve God coming your way and jump aboard. You may well get thrown around, jolted out of your comfort zone and struggle to keep your balance in this new place but as you share the love of Jesus with lost people, you will find your stereotypical Christian life blown apart. What adventure! What joy! Events and opportunities, which break all the stereotypes that you have ever known, will present themselves. Don't be afraid, just 'get into the chariot' and share what God gives you to share.

DEBORAH is a fascinating woman.

She features alongside some real 'cutting edge' chariot-design in Judges 5.

Deborah and Barak have just won a mighty victory for God. They have routed the enemy and to celebrate, they sing 'Deborah's Song'. This is not what Steve Joseph, our Worship Leader at J10, would call a 'Jesus-is-my-girlfriend' type chorus. It contains some pretty sobering information.

Jabin, the King of Canaan, had the most technologically advanced weaponry of the day – 900 iron chariots – with which he oppressed Israel for 20 years. But then, under the leadership of Deborah, the five tribes of Ephraim, Benjamin, Zebulun and Issachar rallied to the cause. They fought hard and won, despite the superior technology against them. But Israel was made up of twelve tribes so what happened to the other seven when they were so desperately needed?

This amazing woman tells us – IN HER SONG!

- Reuben's divisions just talked about fighting (v16) and couldn't make up their minds whether to get involved.
- Gilead played it safe (v17)
- Dan went off sailing (v17)
- Asher just kept his distance from all the trouble (v17).

While some tribes stay away, the 'fighting five' are risking life and limb, defying death as they JUMP IN feet first when invited.

God loves that spirit.

Philip the deacon could have remained a deacon but he became an evangelist in Samaria. He could then have stayed with the revival in Samaria but he was ready for a new challenge – preaching to an Ethiopian in a jolting, creaking, dust-filled, moving wagon

Let me close this chapter with this thought – in a very long sentence.

If the eunuch could engineer the unusual combination of a chariot pulled by oxen instead of horses then the Lord he was seeking could most certainly engineer a Bible Study in a moving pulpit, given by a Holy Spirit-filled deacon, who had come from a 'signs and wonders' revival amongst an ethnic group that his nation hated!

If you are willing to 'get into' all that God has for you, then He can and will also engineer unlikely situations for you too.
Open your mind.
Get ready.
Be prepared to 'get in' and serve Jesus in unlikely places.

Chapter 23

Same Words, Different Motives

While sitting in my holiday home in Mid-Wales, writing this chapter, I was disturbed by the Site Manager. She brought a letter saying that a rabbit cull would take place that evening. The site is overrun with rabbits, literally hundreds of them and for health and safety reasons a pest control company was being brought in to reduce their numbers. They wouldn't be eradicated, just reduced in number. Although they are lovely, fluffy little creatures with their bobbing white tails, I still felt an 'amen' rise from my lips as they have eaten every plant that I have ever planted to beautify my holiday home. The cull was necessary.

God did something similar in the Book of Kings.

God's culling agent was a man called Jehu. He was sent to carry out God's word against Ahab and Jezebel, who you will remember from the Elijah section of this book. In his youth, Jehu had ridden behind Ahab as one of his guards. The Lord directed Elijah to anoint Jehu as future king, a commission which the prophet carried out through his successor Elisha. Jehu was then commissioned to carry out the cull. He was to avenge the blood of Jehovah's prophets and servants on Ahab's whole house.

In modern parlance, Jehu was something of 'a head case'. He was an excitable, impetuous and ambitious character, who without a prayer for guidance, set off to carry out his bloody mission. It was a rough, tough, no holds barred episode in Israel's history.

Just in case you think you have turned over two pages at once or I have lost the plot about the eunuch, Philip and Bible Study, stay with me, please.

While on his mission to slaughter Ahab's whole house, Jehu

met the ascetic Jehonadab. This man was held in universal repute. Jehu wanted his approval for what he's doing and so – just like the eunuch and Philip – he invites Jehonadab up into his chariot. We spent a whole chapter on the eunuch's invitation to Philip to 'get in', now listen to Jehu's words from his war chariot in 2 Kings 10,

"Come with me and see my zeal for the Lord".

'Hey, Jehonadab – get in here and come with me for a ride. I'll show you what a great guy I am and how passionately I serve the Lord!'

Jehu is an ostentatious, murderous hypocrite. He was a show off. His heart was not right with God and the zeal he pretended for the Lord was burning ambition for his own advancement. No-one was going to stand in his way as he climbed the greasy pole to power and glory. His cull of the house of Ahab was not for God's glory but to secure his own succession. His heart couldn't have been more different from that of the eunuch.

Jehu boasted *"Come with me, and see my zeal for the Lord".*

The Ethiopian Chancellor of the Exchequer - in an amazing show of humility and willingness to be taught - was saying, "Come, see my lack of knowledge and instruct me."

These two invitations to 'get in' could not have had more divergent motives. One was to boast, the other was to receive instruction. This is a huge lesson for us to learn. It's not what we say that is important but the motive that lies behind our words. Politicians are not the only ones who say what they think people want to hear – so do Christians. Examination of our motives should be an ongoing process for all of us.

From a distance, looking at these two instances, we see a top-of-the-range chariot stopping on its journey to invite a pedestrian to get in. They do so. Even catching their words would seem to confirm the similarities of the events - the invitation to 'get in'.

However, a 'heart examination' would show huge differences.

A man took his dog to the vets. 'It's dead' said the vet. 'Are you sure?' asked the dog owner, 'could you get a second opinion?' The vet brought in his cat, which sniffed the dead dog and walked out with its tail in the air. Then he brought in his Labrador, which excitedly sniffed the carcass, pushed it with its nose and woofed loudly. 'It is dead' agreed the man.

The vet presented his bill - £250. 'Two hundred and fifty pounds' cried the man, 'to tell me my dog is dead!' 'I would have only charged you £25', explained the vet, 'but the cat scan and the lab test put the price up!' (Sorry!)

God scans our motives. He tests us. What we say isn't so important – it's why we say it. The Ethiopian's 'get in' was a confession of his ignorance and a heart-felt request for instruction in the things of God. Jehu's 'get in' was boastful, arrogant and self-seeking. Same words, diametrically opposed motives. There is humility in the eunuch's words. He is a great man, having risen to the top of government in his own country yet he is ready to listen to Philip the deacon evangelist. The invitation for Philip to climb aboard evidences that.

Over the years I've used a self-made word on many occasions. I believe that a crucial factor in our Christian walk is 'teachability'. As I type this, my computer spell-check has underlined that word but I've ignored it. 'Teachability' is the willingness I have to be taught, trained and advised. Am I willing to receive instruction? Am I willing to invite others into my chariot and say, 'Hey, I don't really understand this! Would you teach me please?'
Jehu was pig-headed, arrogant and boastful. His invitation to

the Man of God was purely self-promotion but the eunuch had 'teachability'. His invitation to the Man of God was genuine. As a result, he learned what the Bible said and came to faith. Very soon, the man is baptized and continuing his long journey home with great joy.

What lies behind our words is life-shaping.

Number of bedrooms in your house, car engine size, the size of your monthly pay-cheque – none of these things are really that important. And like Philip, you may not even own a car.

However, your motives, however, are of the utmost importance.

Here are a few questions to close this Section.

- Would you harness oxen to a chariot?

- When God scans your heart, does He find a willingness to learn?

- When He sends new things your way, do you 'jump in'?

- When unusual combinations are needed, are you stubbornly stereo-typical or flexible?

- When He takes you 'off-roading', do you moan about the jolting or enjoy the challenge?

We could learn a lot from Candace's Chancellor and Phillip the deacon-become-evangelist.

POST SCRIPT

The Eunuch's chariot was most definitely God's wheels because He transformed it into a moving pulpit. For a while, the chariot became a seminar room, a preaching place, God's classroom.

There is something very special about ordinary things which get transformed by God. It may be your favourite armchair that becomes so special because it's while you sit there that God so often speaks to you. It might be a certain walk that you often take, along which the Lord presences Himself quite wonderfully and so for you that piece of geography becomes your meeting ground with the Lord. My caravan in Mid-Wales is such a place. I have spent many prayer days there and heard God on numerous occasions, so it becomes special. In fact, much of this book was written there.

But there is always the danger of making places and things sacred and worshipping them, instead of worshipping the God who meets us there. Congregations begin to treat their meeting places with awe and wonder and then find upgrading or demolishing or moving location almost an impossibility because 'such and such' happened here. The danger is that our history can become our future so nothing changes.

In 2 Kings 18 we find Hezekiah as king of Judah. He did what was right in the eyes of the LORD, just as his forefather David had done. Verse 4 is fascinating because it says,

> *"He removed the high places, smashed the*
> *sacred stones and cut down the Asherah poles.*
> *He broke into pieces the bronze snake Moses*
> *had made, for up to that time the Israelites had*
> *been burning incense to it. (It was called Nehushtan.)"*

The bronze snake made by Moses hundreds of years before, for the people to look at and be healed, had been deified!

139

Instead of melting it down after the plague had passed or putting it in the local museum as a teaching aid for future generations, they gave it a name – Nehushtan – and worshipped it. That is not what God intended for it.

The Eunuch's chariot 'for a while' was God's wheels as Phillip there preached Jesus to him – then it reverted back to being an ox-drawn mode of transport. This post script simply says be aware of 'things' and 'places' that for a time God makes special but don't give them a glory which belongs to God.

They are just 'things'.

Section 7

Revelation's End

Chapter 24

Revelation's End!

The chips, sprinkled with salt and vinegar, lay in a white polystyrene container, which sat on the road map that was balanced on the arm rest and the gear stick. A coffee cup was perched on the dashboard. My right hand held the sandwich box while my left multi-functioned between picking up chips, picking up sandwiches and turning the pages of the Times newspaper which rested on the steering wheel. Wonderful!

The wonder was increased by the view. We had parked roadside in Beaumaris overlooking the Menai Straits, that narrow strip of water which separates Anglesey from Wales. The island was first joined to Wales in 1826 by the Menai Bridge, designed by that architectural and engineering genius, Thomas Telford. That morning, as we motored up through Snowdonia National Park, along the A5, another masterpiece by Telford, I suggested to my navigator that maybe we should go over Telford's suspension bridge rather than the new Britannia Bridge. She nodded in agreement. Always be aware, however, that the devil lies in the detail and in this case, the road we needed to get onto the Menai Bridge lay in the crack of the map. As a result, what seemed so simple became complicated.

Instead of slipping over the bridge, we found ourselves in the backstreets of Bangor. Years of experience and a newfound maturity as I have entered my sixties have taught me to button my lip when these difficulties arise. Harsh words have been spoken in the past on such occasions and my wifely navigator has been forced to retort by uttering words like 'Look, if you are so clever, then you plot your own route...'

Like all men, I am a navigational genius, never needing to ask anyone for advice but we got lost in that navigational black hole, known as the back streets of Bangor. Closely following the sign posts back to the Menai Bridge, we repeatedly found ourselves in the railway station car-park. My levels of patience, lifted to new heights by my newfound maturity, were shrinking by the minute. I thought of Maggie Thatcher's famous words, 'The lady is not for turning ...' as u-turn followed u-turn and I felt ashamed. I just couldn't get my head around a road system that dumps you in a railway station car-park rather than on an historical bridge. Negative thoughts about the competence of the planners were filling my mind and spilling over through my lips.

That all seemed a lifetime away as I ate my chips and read the Times. Newspapers and news bulletins that week were full of Sarah Palin, the Alaskan Governor chosen to be John McCains' running mate in the 2008 American Presidential Election and my newspaper was reporting that she had called Rick Warren of Saddleback Church asking for advice and some Bible verses on how to deal "with the unfair, unjust attacks and the mean-spirited criticism that comes in ...." As a Bible believing Christian, she was under concerted attack by a liberal, God-rejecting media. The media just cannot get their heads around the concept of trusting in an infinite, loving God, who created, maintains and one day will re-create our world.

As I turned the page with my multi-functioning left hand, I read another story about the Royal Society and the Rev Michael Reiss, a biologist and its director of education. He was defending creationism, declaring that it should be taught in our schools to give a more balanced world view. The Royal Society is an august scientific body which counts 21 Nobel Prize winners among its Fellows. His comments 'created' a storm and much controversy. Believing the Bible's account of Creation in Genesis, however you may interpret it, causes great controversy and debate and this was another case of people being unable to get their heads around something. (Reiss was later forced to stand down because of his views.)

**A navigational genius lost in Bangor's station car-park
the media
the Royal Society**

all struggling to get their heads around things that cannot easily be explained

leads me seamlessly onto the Book of Revelation.

From Genesis to Revelation the Bible is controversial.

It is God's account of the past, present and future and as much of our media doesn't believe in God and certainly refuse to contemplate that His word might be true, it causes controversy. Parts of it are difficult to understand and have to be accepted on the basis of simple faith. Sarah Palin was getting the backlash from a media that despises simple faith and also, according to the Times newspaper, was Michael Reiss.

The last book – Revelation - is probably the most difficult of all Bible books to understand, even for Bible-believing followers of Jesus. There have been countless interpretations of just what the Book of Revelation means, some of them differing enormously. Some interpret it in the light of past history; some believe it is future.

Our last chariots are found here.

However, if Ezekiel's wheels were difficult to comprehend, try getting your head around the Apostle John's chariots.

Chapter 25

Apocalypse Future

Jesus Christ came to this planet 2000 years ago at that first Christmas. There were numerous prophecies and predictions about that First Coming but there are even more about his Second Coming. It is obviously in the future because it hasn't yet happened. Many of the events associated with that return, in my understanding, are detailed in the Book of Revelation.

I personally believe that Christ's Second Coming is a two-stage event. Stage One will see millions of Christians disappear in an instant, in the 'twinkling of an eye', at the Rapture of the Church. Stage Two is the 'Glorious Appearing', when Christ comes again after a seven year gap. The seven year gap between those two appearances is called the Tribulation. The verses about the last chariots in the Bible are from that 7 year period. (I fully understand that your views on Revelation could be quite different to mine but stay with the chariots, please!)

The Book of Revelation is the Apostle John's firsthand account of what he saw in a vision unfolding before him. John was 1st century. A person living at the start of the 20th century would have difficulty finding adequate words to describe the awesome effects of the weapons developed over the last hundred years let alone a 1st century man. John uses his words to describe our world.

Into this context and restriction of vocabulary, we encounter our final chariots, found in the first verses of chapter 9.

> *"The fifth angel sounded his trumpet ....*
> *The locusts looked like horses prepared for battle.*
> *On their heads they wore something like crowns of gold, and their faces resembled human faces. Their hair was like women's hair, and their teeth were*

like lions' teeth.

They had breastplates like breastplates of iron, and the sound of their wings was like the thundering of many horses and chariots rushing into battle. They had tails and stings like scorpions, and in their tails they had power to torment people for five months"

'Been there, seen it, done it and got the tee-shirt' is a commonly used phrase. There's not much that surprises us 21st century people. We are more widely travelled than any generation before us, thanks to cheap airline travel. We have seen most things on our planet, through the medium of TV if not directly. Choices unimaginable to our forbears mean that we can experience a whole range of things. Our t-shirt motifs list the places visited, things experienced and slogans about ourselves. Smugness is a facet of 21st century living and everything we encounter can be explained.

We can get our heads around everything!

Things that go bump in the night, ghosts and unquiet spirits are researched using the latest technical equipment.

The Large Hadron Collider has sent its protons off on their dizzying journey through time and space, close to the speed of light, generating new physics and looking for black holes and the 'God' particle.

Upturns and downturns in the economy have explanations as we battle inflation, recession and stagflation, negative equity, gazumping and gazundering.

All we need to know about our physical and mental traits can be found in our DNA.

Our experts can explain everything!
That creates a problem, however, when we come to God.

Neither our experts nor our scientists nor our religious leaders can explain Him and his works. And neither can you and I. Man cannot get its head around the Almighty. It requires simple faith – and that's where we began this final section with Sarah Palin and a cynical media.

The 'wheels' in the first sections of this book were simple, weren't they? A wooden frame with two or four wheels, pulled by oxen or horses is within the scope of anyone's understanding. Unfortunately, the wheels at the end of this book are anything but simple.

> *"They had breastplates like breastplates of iron, and the sound of their wings was like the thundering of many horses and chariots rushing into battle. They had tails and stings like scorpions, and in their tails they had power to torment people for five months".*

Just for the record, I think that these 'scorpions' are modern fighter aircraft. They have wings; they sound like chariots going into battle which is all John would know; they had tails and could sting like scorpions – missiles or gunfire. Whether that is correct or incorrect is relatively unimportant. These verses in Revelation take us into Biblical prophetic revelation that we cannot easily get our heads around. There are no simple, obvious explanations.

I did a year-long study with my church on the Book of Revelation and many cassette and CD copies of those studies were distributed because people found them fascinating. However, I began that teaching series with this proviso – the studies were my interpretation of the Book, utilizing the research and suggestions and teachings of much greater Bible students than I. However, my explanation of those chapters could be wrong.

The last lesson from 'God's Wheels' is very simple yet profound.

God wants to take us to a level where we trust Him although we don't fully understand. Even when we can't explain facts, events, the happenings of life, we are still confident in our God. Just because we cannot get our head around some things, our heart still responds to His love.

Each of us operates on a different intellectual plain and some have greater understanding than others of facts and principles and natural laws. However, you will never get your head round God. It requires your heart. Whatever these chariots were, seen by the Apostle John in his vision, our inability to tie them down, define them, exegete these verses with unwavering accuracy, should not deter us from trusting the One, who gave John a glimpse of them.

Chapter 25

Time and Eternity

The singing of the choir filled the nave of Chester cathedral, as intricate harmonies, major and minor, wove together. My soul soared with their voices. As they sang, I observed the huge pillars and vaulted ceilings high above me and they made me feel very small. Then creeping into my mind came the thought that in this place, men and women had been worshipping the Lord for hundreds and hundreds of years. I felt even smaller. The words of a verse from an old hymn confirmed my smallness:

> Time like an ever rolling stream,
> Bears all its sons away;
> They fly forgotten as a dream
> Dies at the opening day.

The thousands who had worshipped in that place over the centuries were forgotten – time saw to that. Time erases memories. The TV programme 'Who do you think you are?' shows the rich and famous unaware of their predecessors even from two or three generations ago. We are quickly forgotten except for a few outstanding individuals. As the choir continued to sing, I felt that I wasn't even small, I was just nothing, a passing breath in the relentless march of time. And Peter's words came to me, words often quoted at funerals.

> *"All flesh is as grass,*
> *And all the glory of man as the flower of the grass.*
> *The grass withers,*
> *And its flower falls away .... "*

It wasn't depression or melancholia that I was feeling as these thoughts chased each other through my mind – it was reality. A true sense of perspective was being formed in my thinking. The Apostle Peter, in the previous verse, had been contrasting that which is produced by man with that which is produced by God, with reference to its permanency. The former is corruptible and decaying; the latter abiding. There is no stability in anything that man does or produces. He resembles grass that soon fades and withers or as the hymn writer puts it a 'dream that dies when the new day opens'.

But, of course, my quotations from Peter – and the hymn writer – are incomplete.

> *"All flesh is as grass,*
> *And all the glory of man as the flower of the grass.*
> *The grass withers,*
> *And its flower falls away,*
> *But the word of the LORD endures forever."*

"The word of the Lord endures forever" and in that Word I have put my trust and in its author my confidence rests. My spirit has been infused by His Holy Spirit and I have a permanence which is eternal.

These thoughts were flying through my mind in nano-seconds.

The choir was still singing as I journeyed down to an ever-increasing sense of my smallness and then took flight again as I embraced a fresh realization of just who I am as I recalled the words of Peter a little earlier in that chapter:

> *"Praise be to the God and Father of our Lord*
> *Jesus Christ! In his great mercy he has given us*
> *new birth into a living hope through the resurrection*
> *of Jesus Christ from the dead, and into an inheritance*
> *that can never perish, spoil or fade – kept in heaven for*
> *you, who through faith are shielded by God's power until*
> *the coming of the salvation that is ready to be revealed*
> *in the last time".*1 Peter 1:3

I may be a 'nobody', forgotten even by my own family in two or three generations and small in relation to the soaring pillars of the cathedral - but I have an incorruptible inheritance. The Word of God, which I have believed, has birthed something in me which is eternal. The choir finished singing as the words of another verse of the hymn slipped into place:

> 'O God our help in ages past,
> Our hope for years to come.
> A shelter from the stormy blast,
> And our eternal home'.

Time reduces all of us to a memory. But one day, in the future, I will step out of time and into eternity. The Lord Jesus whom I have loved and served for most of my life will welcome me. He lives in an eternal now.

Right now, I am sorry to tell you, dear reader, that I cannot fully get my head around John's horses and chariots. They might indeed be modern fighter aircraft or, as one commentator suggests, Saracens from a former age. It doesn't get much more diverse in explanation than that, does it?

Fortunately, I don't need to understand the poetic language of the Apocalypse. I don't need a detailed explanation. I only need the God who created time. He has helped me in the past and will never leave me in the future. He is my hope. This same writer, John, in his gospel quoted Jesus when he said that he was going to prepare an eternal home for me. When I get there, one of these days, I will ask Him,

'Lord – these chariots that you showed to your friend, John the Apostle, what ARE they?'

Until then – I'll let them pass.

Chapter 27

Journey's End

I set out at the beginning of this book to see if there was link between someone so infinite and majestic and glorious as our God – and something as mundane, finite and varied in style as 'wheels'. Was it was possible, in different ways, to 'love' them both?

To try and answer that question, I have shared with you the verses that I stumbled across as I read my Bible which could indicate that my amazing Lord might understand my fascination with 'wheels'. I truly hope that you have enjoyed our journey together.

I asked a dear friend, Rose Till, one of my associate pastors for many, many years at J10, to read the first draft of this book. She made a number of helpful comments, particularly one about 'leaving too many loose ends untied!' So let me tie up some loose ends.

CHURCH

In April 2008, 30 years after planting the church with just 8 people, I handed over the leadership of the church to another of my associate pastors, a fine young man called Jonathan Bentley. I am still on Staff and firmly rooted into Junction 10 but God spoke very clearly to me as I considered transitioning the church to my successor. 'You have poured 30 years into ONE church; now all that experience and wisdom you have acquired is to be shared across many, many other churches and fellowships .... '

I am now doing this.

Part of the outworking of this 'word' was the establishing of 'Network Central', a friendship / help group for leaders of smaller churches. Together with Judith and the 'Magnificent Seven', we are ministering into 18/20 other local churches – and some not so local. The 'Magnificent Seven' are a group of retired or resting leaders plus a couple of younger guys with a combined total of about 300 years experience in local church. We are a very mixed bunch but great friends and passionate about helping other leaders and their fellowships. The 'Seven' certainly break down the usual stereotypes about leaders.

When introducing the 'Seven' to our first gathering of Network Central leaders, I gave them just 2 minutes to say a bit about themselves. Big Bob, an elder at J10 for many years, as part of his introduction said, "I have been happily married for 30 years. Last month we celebrated our 40th wedding anniversary!" The place collapsed in laughter.

We do laugh a lot. Too many Christian leaders take themselves far too seriously and forget that "*a cheerful heart does good like medicine*" (Proverbs 17:22). We also weep together, pray together and encourage one another in the work of God. Network Central is a 'work in progress'.

About midway through my 30 years leading J10, Clive Calver of the Evangelical Alliance came to preach for us. I was a little surprised when he accepted our invitation as he was a very busy man but he did say that he wanted to spend the Sunday afternoon with me as he had something to say? Sitting in my office, he began to question me – 'How many people were there on staff? How many of my hours were paid for by the church?' He asked many similar questions. The answer to all his questions was 'None!'

Then he explained.

'I was working down the road in Wolverhampton, John, when you planted this church in 1978. I was with a young man called Graham Kendrick. I've watched from afar your progress and growth. It's been quite dramatic. (It never seemed dramatic to us, just steady growth and hard work! However, he then gave me some statistics about where we came in terms of comparable growth over that period. I was pleasantly surprised.) But, unless you take on some staff, go onto staff yourself – at least part-time – you will burn out!'

It was sound advice which I accepted, although amazed that he knew of us from our earliest days. Since then, our Staff has steadily grown and God has blessed us with so many wonderful people. Junction 10 Church has truly been a team effort. Currently we have 5 full-time staff plus 3 part-time plus lots of volunteers. We couldn't manage the 600/700 people that God has entrusted to us without our army of volunteers. Like any other church, J10 is also 'a work in progress' - growing and developing and changing to meet the needs of our 21st century society. It's in fresh hands now but the God who has brought us thus far, will surely continue to bless us.

FRIENDS

The greatest thing in life is good friends. I wouldn't for one moment consider mentioning any of ours by name for fear of missing someone out – they are just too numerous – but they know who they are. They are some of God's greatest gifts to us.

FAMILY

Anna, our daughter, is just a great woman of God. Whenever I need prayer support, she is someone to whom I turn. After years of rebellion, she came back to the Lord and is using much of what she experienced during her 'wilderness years', to help others. Working for Black Country Connexions, she has a client list of around 20 young people who are either in, just out of, or going to prison. She truly has found her 'niche' ministry.

Mark is a school teacher, teaching in a primary school, for

which he is an absolute 'natural'. Like his mom, he is a brilliant musician, using his skills both in church and in school. His cancer is many years behind him. Thank you, Lord!

Mark is married to Lydia, who is training to be a nurse. She is the perfect daughter-in-law.

These three – Mark, Anna and Lydia – are among my greatest friends. Whenever I need help, encouragement or just some fun, these top my list. If I need to confide in someone or need advice, I turn to these three. They are incomparable.

I never thought I could love anyone as much as our kids but then along came Luke and James, our grandsons. They are the absolute light of our lives. Rolling around on the floor, playing football, fighting with light sabres or reading stories, it's brought a whole new dimension into our lives. What joy!

And finally, I think you've 'got the picture' about Judith as you've read the book.

> *"An excellent wife, who can find?*
> *For her worth is far above jewels.*
> *The heart of her husband trusts in her,*
> *And he will have no lack of gain.*
> *She does him good and not evil*
> *All the days of her life..... "*   Proverbs 31:10-12

God in His foresight knew how much help this car-mad male from Lower Gornal, with no Bible College training, was going to need to plant and pastor the Church at Junction 10. He also knew that he would need lots of love and encouragement and womanly wisdom. He would also need a partner who wouldn't complain when life was tough, unfair and so demanding.
His answer was Judith.
Enough said!

AND FINALLY - THE CAR?

If you ever go into my garage, up one corner, attached to the door are many, many number plates. They represent just a fraction of the cars I have had. Towing a caravan and garden trailer meant that I always had to get a spare number plate and when I sold the car, I kept the plate. Cars have been my weakness I suppose, a possibility strongly endorsed by my long-suffering wife!

From that first Mini with the go-slower engine, I have driven Volvos, Jaguars, Range Rovers, Discoverys, Renaults, Peugeots and just one Austin Montego Estate. Currently, I'm driving a 1.5dci Renault Scenic – my fifth.

Lust for more expensive cars has now abated. Only very occasionally do I get a flicker of yearning for something bigger / faster / sleeker / different but then 'common sense' takes over .... ?

So let me finish with the verse that began this journey.

> *"There is no one like the God of Jeshurun, who*
> *Rides the heavens to help you ..... "*

God wants to take us to a level where we trust Him although we don't fully understand. Even when we can't explain facts, events, the happenings of life, we can still be confident in our God. Just because we cannot get our head around some things, our heart still responds to His love.

Wherever you go, whatever you drive - may the God who rides the heavens, ride with you!

POST SCRIPT

How on earth can we justify these last chariots from the Book of Revelation a place in our book? These are most definitely NOT God's wheels! In fact, we don't even see them, just hear them. They 'sounded' like "the thundering of many horses and chariots rushing into battle" so I could be walking on thin ice by including them.

However – (I love using that word and it's the last time I will use it in this book) – I have one final thing to tell you. It's time to let you in on a secret. When I wrote this book, I had to write an explanation for possible publishers as to just why I wrote it. Let me quote to you from that explanation:

'I have noted many things over 30 years as a pastor. One thing I have sadly noted is that not too many Christian men read books. Wives / girlfriends usually read them and tell their husband / boyfriend what they've read but only a minority of men (usually leaders) read books.

I've also noted that many Christian men are interested in cars / bikes / transport. They are happy to read car magazines, watch TV motoring programmes, talk to mates about their cars and take walks around car showrooms.

Would it be possible, by using that interest in 'wheels' to get Christian men to read a book about 'wheels' in the Bible, which then teaches on a whole range of things? This book is that attempt. It is primarily aimed for men, but women will love reading it (I think!). It may be that a woman will buy it, read it and urge her partner to read it too.

The subjects covered are wide and varied, ranging from the first carts, tabernacle worship, a 'cow miracle', the Bible's cleverest chariot dealer, God taking out Elijah out in a chariot of fire and off-roading with the Ethiopian eunuch. We end in Revelation trying to 'get our heads around' Apocalyptic chariots!'

It just may be that you are – were – one of those people who rarely read Christian books. Now here you are, on the final Post Script, after dipping with me into the Book of Revelation. Your whole horizon will have shifted because we have touched on a huge range of subjects and ideas and dreams. I have said things that you agreed with, disagreed with, made you smile and hopefully, challenged you to a closer walk with Jesus. You may even recommend this book to another 'non-reading' friend. My prayer for you is that you will continue to read widely.

Although I cannot strictly justify the Revelation sound of chariots in a book called 'God's Wheels', IF THEY HAVE TAUGHT YOU THAT YOU CANNOT GET YOUR HEAD AROUND EVERYTHING AND SOME THINGS HAVE TO BE ACCEPTED IN SIMPLE FAITH, then they truly are God's wheels!